UNMASKING THE CULT MENTALITY

(An Exposition)

By
Rayola Kelley

Hidden Manna Publications

Unmasking the Cult Mentality
Rayola Kelley, Copyright © 2006 and 2025

GENTLE SHEPHERD MINISTRIES
www.gentleshepherd.com

ISBN: 979-8-9994555-4-3

Except where otherwise indicated, all Scripture quotations in this book are taken from the King James Version of the Bible.

Hidden Manna Publications
P.O. Box 3572
Oldtown, ID 83822
www.gentleshepherd.com

Facebook:
https://www.facebook.com/HiddenMannaPublications/

Contents

Bonus Book

HE ACTUALLY THOUGHT IT NOT ROBBERY

INTRODUCTION

Questions, questions, and more questions continue to flood the minds of those who have tasted the bitterness of a cult. Often bound together by a common religious experience, these individuals find themselves struggling with the same issues. It seems that even after being delivered from their cult's tentacles, they have more doubts than answers. How do they handle a situation where they have been subjected to religious people who have ended up betraying them? In fact, some people would classify their experience as spiritual abuse. Granted, there are hurts and unresolved issues, but what continues to nip at these people's heels comes in the way of suspicions and doubts as to what is true and real.

Religious people had these poor sincere victims' trust, but they used it to promote their own means. These imposters had these individuals' loyalty, but they used it to control these innocent receptive souls. They not only had a hold on these people hearts, but they stomped on them through fear and manipulation. They clearly had the attention of their followers' ears, but they had cleverly perverted and poisoned what they told these people, thereby, changing their perspective.

For these poor followers, doubts and questions continue to grow even after time and space has marked their separation from their religious experience. Questions such as how could such leaders be under the right spirit if they were operating according to wickedness (*Isaiah 25:7; 30:1; 1 John 4:1*)? If they were being influenced by a wrong spirit, how did this spirit affect their understanding of God and what they perceive as

Christianity? If the leaders were in error and operating according to it, how much of their teachings were trustworthy?

The one ray of hope out of this is that some of these poor abused souls have concluded that in spite of their religious experience, they still want God. Sadly, there are many people that walk away from God when their religious leaders or experiences fail them.

However, God is distinct from man and religion. But, where do such individuals begin in their search for the true God of heaven? How do they discern between the influence of heretical religious leaders and that of truth and righteousness? Who can begin to help these individuals come to terms with the issues that loom before them? After all, they are now suspicious of all religious people. They have seen the insidious control of leaders with personal agendas, riding high on ego trips, but the one question that haunts them is whether there is one person who is willing to step up to the plate to help them wade through the maze of deception without seeking brownie points or personal victories. Is there such a person who will not take advantage of their vulnerability, while being patient with their suspicions? Is there someone who will not be judgmental when it comes to all of their questions and fear of being deceived again?

Clearly these individuals need a revelation of Jesus Christ. But, who can they trust or where can they go to find the space to work through the spiritual and emotional devastation that they must now wade through to come back to the center of truth? They clearly need to be constructively challenged by truth that will set them free.

This book is designed to help Christians understand the debate that rages in the minds of those who have a cult mentality. It is vital that we who claim fundamental ties to the Christian faith have the means to give an account of the hope that is in us. It is this hope that can only be realized in the life and truth of Christ that will wonderfully and gloriously set these people free from their cult mentality.

In order to bring a better understanding of this subject, I have included a bonus book to complement this information. Since the main test of the kingdom of God comes down to one's perspective of God, the book, *He Thought it Not Robbery,* has been included in this exposition. The real test brings one back to if they believe God is the Great I AM, Creator of all, and who they say and believe Jesus Christ is. (See *1 Timothy 3:16* and *Ephesians 5:30-32.*)

Section 1

ESTABLISHING A STANDARD OF TRUTH

THRESHOLD
OF ETERNITY

I wrote the exposition about the cult mentality back in 2006. At that time, I was contending with people who came out of a cult that taught against the deity of Christ. As I observed these people, they referred to, and used, the Jesus who was erected in their mind in terms of simply being a "good" man. In their thinking He had become a martyr, but was void of deity and the power of the eternal. I recognized that like their Jesus, they had no real authority to stand and no power to overcome.

The greatest attack against the fundamental beliefs of the Christian is against the person and identity of Jesus Christ. The Lord Jesus Christ is deity, eternal in nature, and due to the eternal plan of the Father, He took on humanity to become the perfect sacrifice that could satisfy the judgment of the law on all sin. In His humanity He secured redemption, and in His deity He possessed resurrection power to overcome the enemy of all mankind, death.[1]

The attack against Jesus' deity can be found in most cults. Many declare He is a created being rather than the Creator.[2] Granted, in many cases Jesus, in His humanity, is exalted in some fashion by them, but He has clearly been stripped of His deity in subtle ways. We see this in the fiction book, *The Shack* and in some of the media presentations such as "*The Chosen.*" These presentations are slowly re-imagining a god that many

---

[1] John 1:1-3; 2:19-21; Romans 10:4
[2] Colossians 1:15-18

can relate to, a god that has been humanified to fit in with their fickle sentiment and limited understanding.

Those who are sentimentally caught up with these presentations fail to discern how Jesus is not being presented Scripturally. The unveiling of Jesus as to His dual natures is a matter of revelation and not intellectual deduction. In some cases, those who see some discrepancy in such presentations shrug it off, thinking it is not all that important because it is just a matter of those in charge taking some liberties with the Bible and the person of Jesus. Since these individuals perceive they know the truth, they conclude they will keep it straight. However, the problem is that wrong presentations slowly dull people's discernment down to the point that nothing contrary to God's holiness is really all that bad.[3] There is no real urgency to ensure the integrity of truth.

If that is not enough, many of the Bible versions use pronouns when it comes to Jesus. Don't get me wrong there are versions that adjust Jesus to some cultural agenda and are an abomination to God, but in other cases where the version is acceptable to many Christians, Jesus is identified with a pronoun.

The Savior of the world is more than a mere pronoun. He is the Son of God, the Son of Man, the Promised Messiah, and the King of kings and Lord of lords to name a few of His titles. These are names that identify Him to His nature, His authority, and His Work, and to render Him into a simple pronoun is to make Him common, and when the things of God are made common it is blasphemous to Him. Such as in the case of the sons of Aaron who treated what God had ordained as being sacred as common which resulted in judgment.[4]

Who Jesus is, is what serves as our only true foundation. Without this sure foundation, people have no Rock to anchor to

---

[3] Matthew 13:15-16; John 16:13; 1 John 2:27
[4] Leviticus 10:1-3

and they become like corks on the ocean who can be cleverly taken by every wind of doctrine that comes through Christendom.[5]

The plight of man has also been watered down. Even though man is dead in sin, there are those who, like the Unitarians, believe that there is some good in man that can be salvaged and he will come out better for it, even though the Bible states there is no good thing in man. Then there are the Universalists who believe all mankind can be saved regardless of whether or not they enter the narrow way of Christ's redemption. The latest is Universal Reconciliation that believes somehow even Satan will be given a second chance in order to be reconciled back to the Creator.[6]

As a Christian, I have witnessed the disaster of the occultic "Seed Faith," that merged into "Positive Confession" where man dictates to God by twisting His arm with His promises or declarations. There is also Kingdom Dominion where man will usher in the kingdom of heaven and not Jesus. These waves have opened the way for many false prophets to ride high on their heresies. In some circles it is taught that these elite can work their way into immortality. Even today some of these beliefs have merged into a movement where man perceives he will usher in the thousand years of peace. Jesus' name is used but there is no mention of His salvation, and the Word is quoted but much of it, especially concerning the last days, are cast aside such as the return of Jesus to set up HIS kingdom.[7]

As one who has been saved out of a prominent cult and has been involved in the ministry for over four decades, I have watched with my co-laborer of 35 years many movements flow in, through and out of Christendom. I must state there is only One true movement that must occur within the Church, through the

---

[5] 1 Corinthians 3:11; Ephesians 4:14
[6] Isaiah 64:6; Romans 3:23; 6:23; 7:18; Hebrews 9:27
[7] Matthew 24:30-31; Revelation 19:11-20:6

Body, and overflow to affect others eternally, and that is the move of the Holy Spirit upon hearts and minds. Any movement, no matter how pious, good, or sincere it may look, if the true Holy Spirit is not present, it will take people past the shorelines of safety and out into the dangerous ocean of delusion and judgment.[8]

We know in the end days that God is sending a wave of strong delusion to test and judge hearts. The Apostle Paul warned that in the last days there will be seducing spirits and doctrines of demons abounding. Jesus warned that the deception would be so great that if it was possible the elect would be deceived. Only those who love the truth of who God is and what His Son has done will survive the great testing of this delusion.[9]

Initially, some of the past movements were recognized for what they were and rejected by many fundamental leaders, but the problem is that each wave has subtly reshaped the environment of the church. These subtle changes have conditioned the upcoming generation to become more susceptible to the repackaged lies that ride high on various popular waves that include powerful experiences, so-called "new spirituality," greater enlightenment, and dark powers that come across as light, but lack the real light of the world, Jesus.[10]

My first encounter with these doctrines of demons was in High School where I was taught evolution. Evolution is the foundation of the atheistic religion of humanism which serves as the main religion of Communism. At best, it is a shaky theory that hides behind scientific declarations that have been disproven by such things as the protein (amino acid) chain and DNA. However, we now have people who declare science is their trustworthy savior, while Jesus is nothing but a myth and that

---

[8] Zechariah 4:6
[9] Matthew 24:24; 2 Thessalonians 2:10-12; 1 Timothy 4:1
[10] John 8:12; 9:5

there is no God. They use science to label every sin as a disorder or illness instead of the grave spiritual, deadly cancer it is to the soul.

Since humanism exalts man in some way, its godless philosophy of psychology has replaced the wisdom and counsel of God's Word, while self-esteem and self-love become the mantra of the times. All man has to do to change his life is love himself a little more.

As Christians, we are told that our affections must be set on the things of heaven and not on the earth. Our love for anything on this earth, including family, must pale in comparison when it comes to our love for God. As the Bible states, we can only serve one master at a time, and we serve what we believe and choose to love. It is only God's selfless, sacrificial love that reveals what true love is, and the one characteristic that sets it apart is the denial of self in order to prefer the welfare of others over ourselves.[11]

Humanism purports that only the fittest will survive; therefore, abortion and euthanasia of the vulnerable, weak, and elderly is logical. In some arenas abortions are exposed as being nothing but sacrifices to Satan who demands the blood of the innocent from his followers. We witnessed many of these diabolical practices during Hitler's regime as he deemed Jews less than human, giving him a right in his mind to experiment with them and murder them. These different selfisms are definitely contrary to denying oneself in order to follow Jesus away from the godless influences and rudiments of this fallen world that knows nothing but anger, learns war, hates what does not fit, and prefers death.[12]

Now everything is relative and nothing is absolute. The Bible is clear; truth is eternal and will stand when all else collapses.[13]

---

[11] Matthew 6:24; 10:37-39; John 3:16; Romans 12:9-10; Colossians 3:2
[12] Proverbs 8:36; Isaiah 2:4; Matthew 16:24-26; Colossians 2:8
[13] 2 Corinthians 13:8

Diversity is another mantra of the times where everyone must embrace everything in the name of Political Correctness to prove we are reasonable and loving people. DEI is the agenda where all morality is stomped into the ground and abominable practices are taught as "normal" and flaunted in people's faces. All order and sanity are being cast to the side, while true science is being shelved as mankind is being told he can change his gender, his nature, his kind, and his order so he can live as he will and do as he will.

All these heretical, godless presentations are so entangled with each other, that they create a gigantic dead tree with entwined branches in a dark forest that captures anyone who dares to wander off from what is true or arrogantly seek a way through it. It is important to point out that even in this chapter's presentation of such heresy, it is just the tip of the iceberg and that its evil depths reach into hell.

In the days of the Apostle John there was Gnosticism. That is what he was combatting in his first epistle. Gnostics believe in seeking spiritual enlightenment and they conveniently separate the body from the soul. They believe the soul is good, but the body is bad because it is in the body that bad things occur.

Today the same separation exists. Consider the statement, "God hates the sin, but loves the sinner." This is a Gnostic concept. Yes, God loves us but each of us will be judged for our deeds that we have done in the body. If the soul is found wanting because it has not been redeemed by the blood of the Lamb, it will end up in hell, not the body. We need to remember we are sinners because we sin.[14]

Enlightenment lays at the heart of many cults, which includes secret societies such as the Freemasons, as well as Eastern Mysticism within the New Age Movement and Hinduism. This

---

[14] Matthew 10:28; Romans 5:6-10

enlightenment finds it source in the great lie of Satan in the garden that man "can be as gods."[15]

When it comes to Western thinking, secularism and not religion is the preference. Those who thought themselves wise in their own eyes became disenchanted towards religion. They blamed the misery of man on the restrictions and disciplines of religion. Although man was formed to reflect the image of his Creator, these high-minded fools perceived that man could remake himself.[16] They even presented a road map as to how to achieve this paradigm. They knew that it would take crises and social disruption to drive such changes. Hence enters Re-Enchantment.

These godless individuals knew that secularization is always the intermediate stage between a religious society on the way out and the appearance of a new religious structuring. This new structuring has to do with Socialism and Progressivism where changes must and can progress forward in the society. This requires man to be the answer to what ails mankind, ever willing to sacrifice "all" for the "common good" of humanity. He must solve the problems by being his brother's keeper by taking care of the social ills of society. This allows those in power to steal by taking from the rich, redistributing it to the poor while bringing everyone down to utter poverty so no one feels they are missing out or inferior to the masses. This type of environment, for a time, allows the do-gooders to feel good about themselves, thinking they indeed can make the world better. What came out of this movement was the "social gospel," that saves no one and a "social justice" that is void of real justice.

Consider the actual Age of Enlightenment. Men in high places, who did not want to believe God, devised this age to lure others into it. It was during great upheaval, such as the French

---

[15] Genesis 3:5
[16] Psalm 14:1; 53:1; Romans 8:29

Revolution, that this took center stage. After all, Christianity offered heaven but the world had nothing to offer.

Hence entered this Age of Enlightenment. Man needed to see how he could save himself and devise his own utopia here, whether it be Camelot, the beautiful city on a hill, or even the American Dream; all he needed was to be enlightened to see his potential. Part of this age of enlightenment was the promise of man entering into a "golden age." The purpose of the age of enlightenment was to destroy any witness of the Light of the world and the hope of heaven and make man the savior.[17]

Out of the Age of enlightenment came critical thinking that took hold of the colleges where man became the one who decided what was valid when it came to Christianity and God's Word. It was followed by the New Age movement that encouraged man to find the divine within himself, to recognize the Christ consciousness. From man's mental ascent to deity came such things as "Pantheism" that the universe is God, and "Oneness" where we are all one in sameness and identity. It also teaches that God reveals Himself in various forms which was promoted by the book, "*The Shack.*"

The goal of major cults is to take over the world and rule it with their form of religion. Hindus started this takeover in the 1970s. They knew that the environment was right because a spiritual vacuum existed due to the disillusionment of many in the western world. The gurus knew by introducing it as science (biofeedback), as exercise (Yoga—linking with demons), healthy holistic practices as spiritual enlightenment and so forth that many would wander into their dark tenacles seeking light at the tree of worldly knowledge that contained the deadly seeds of deception. These practices promised to change "bad karma" that plagued people and to deliver them out of the endless cycle or reincarnation.

---

[17] John 9:4-5

Although drugs could quickly usher people into an altered reality, proponents of being enlightened also knew meditation was another effective passageway into the spiritual realm. This practice has now graduated into contemplative prayer. This is where one opens their mind to the unseen world to have a spiritual encounter; therefore, allowing any spirit guide of the New Age or the many gods (demons) of Hinduism to come in and give them the power they seek and experiences they want, in order to come out with a sense of greater spirituality.

These different movements of trying to bring the holy into agreement with the unholy, profaning what is true was being pushed by ecumenicalism.[18] This movement's goal has always been to bring the religious world under one umbrella, but since there are so many, which one of the religious institutions or movements will come out of top?

For centuries the Catholic church has been trying to make the world Catholic. As mentioned, the Hindus made their inroads into the psyche of societies in the 1970s, but now we have the Muslims who are trying to invade every political arena in the western world with Islam.

They are in many ways being effective in pushing their concept of their god, Allah (the pagan moon god of Mesopotamia) and their Sharia Law on an environment that has conditioned the sheep to be led to the slaughter. They offer their paradise and their idea of the Messiah, Maitreya. Their demands are simple, bow to both their god and law and live, or die as an "infidel." Today there is even an unholy mixture of Christianity and Islam. It is called, Chrislam.

It is clear that a one-world religion is emerging, but the overseer of it will be none of the vying religions that are trying to rule the world. It is evident that we are living in perilous times as we witness the dangerous slope of technology promoting avatars

---

[18] 2 Corinthians 6:14-18

(incarnation of oneself), bringing about transhumanism where knowledge of God will be programed out of man, and now turning everything, especially our economic system, over to artificial intelligence. This is why it is important to understand how the environment of the church was conditioned in such a way that it has become unrecognizable from the first Church that was established in the New Testament.

It is important to note that hell will not prevail against the true Church, the body of Christ, but there is a visible representation of the church that is organized and part of Satan's systems. Sadly, the voice of the Shepherd is not being heard in many of these institutions, causing the sheep to scatter to find good pasturelands and living water.[19]

The reason that the battle has been great for hearts and minds is that the deception comes from one source, Satan, the god of this world who seeks worship. This age is under his spirit that works disobedience in the hearts of people towards God. The roots of it go back to the Tower of Babel where man was striving to climb higher than God to humble Him, and take charge. When man is involved in anti-God religion, it will be rendered into decadent paganism that will be flaunted in God's face. Like the leader and founder of Babel, Nimrod, who was a hunter of men's souls, the false religious leaders of today are trying to snatch souls to gain a following, an army that will take God down from His throne so man can call the shots and rule his own destiny.[20]

And, where are the shepherds who are to oversee the Lord's sheep? As in the case of Jude, those who were to oversee the welfare of the church were unaware of the dangers that were creeping in among the sheep.[21] Perhaps they were assuming that the sheep would certainly see the error.

---

[19] Jeremiah 23:1-2; Matthew 16:18; John 10:3-5
[20] Genesis 10:8-10; 11:1-9; John 8:44; 2 Corinthians 4:3-4; Ephesians 2:2
[21] Jude 1-4

In our case, we can see how each movement proved to be more subtle and enticing. These movements sounded logical, seemed religious enough, spouted enough "Christianeze" terminology that it sounded right, and sadly received enough backing by silent Christian leaders who did not seem alarmed by the teachings of the imposters to disciple, instruct, and warn the sheep.

In spite of the failure of shepherds to warn God's sheep and prepare them to stand against deception, the people have God's Word. Past prophets have been warning us about the times we live in, and there are many books exposing the heresy, but if the people are failing to hear the warnings and instructions, it is because they are dull of hearing or they do not want to hear.[22] In the end, there will be no excuse for them not knowing the true score.

We are not here to live our lives as we see fit; rather, we are here to be living, walking, talking witnesses of God. To be a living witnesses in this dark world, the first Church had to be established upon the right foundation and lined up to the only true Cornerstone, Jesus Christ. This was the only means for it to become the sound structure in the midst of ongoing storms and battles that would continually confront it in the world that hates God, shuns His redemption, and persecutes His followers. There are plenty of books about heresy, but one main book about what is true when it comes to God—the Holy Bible.

You might ask, why make a big deal out of this issue? It is because man stands on the threshold of eternity and when the door opens, he will find himself in the glorious presence of God or in the holding place of hell. In hell he has nothing to look

---

[22] There are many good resources and books about these godless movements and beliefs such as *Game of Gods* by Carl Teichrib, *A Time of Departing* by Ray Yungen, *Occult Invasion* by Dave Hunt to name a few. Good sources in which you can obtain valuable information on these various subjects is the Berean Call, Lighthouse Trails Publishing, and on Islam, Shahram Hadian's ministry, Truth In Love Project.

forward to except that great day of judgment, where he will stand before his great Judge without any defense for his wickedness and unbelief, no recourse in which to seek any type of pardon, and no hope for he has rejected the only hope of glory beyond this world and hell that he was ever offered, the Lord Jesus Christ. [23]

THE FOUNDATION

As Christians who must contend for the faith that was first delivered to the saints, we need to understand how to help those with a cult mentality.[24] Needless to say, such people must be open to honestly evaluate the shaky foundation and pseudo faith they might still be clinging to due to the influence of their cult. Clearly, these individuals must have a contrast with which to compare, consider, and separate heresy from truth. But, before these individuals can bring a separation through reasoning at the point of Scripture, they must first come to terms with what they believe.

In order to expose their right belief system, the right questions must be asked. But what are the right questions, especially if you are not sure about what to ask? After all, these individuals may possess some right beliefs that have been cleverly laced with wrong influences and teachings. Or, perhaps they have been exposed to a wrong spirit, while much of their foundation would prove to be stable. On the other hand, maybe their whole foundation is wrong.

The key is foundation. Unsuspecting people test all matters according to the foundation that has been established. If people have a wrong foundation, then nothing they believe will stand under scrutiny or judgment. Therefore, the first challenge to these people's mentality must be taken from *Matthew 7:24-27.*

---

[23] Luke 16:19-31; Colossians 1:27; Revelation 20:11-15
[24] Jude 3

What has their foundation been established upon, the sand of man's ever-changing religion or has it been founded upon the Rock of ages?

Wrong spiritual foundations are often made up of presumptions and assumptions or truths and righteous doctrines. The dictionary states that a presumption is an attitude or belief dictated by probability.[25] In other words, a person presumes that they understand a matter based on an assumption. Assumptions or assumed beliefs are comprised of an understanding or belief that the individual assumes is true, but which has never really been personally tested. When an assumed belief is challenged, a person can become confused, angry, and fearful. Peter challenged such assumptions in *1 Peter 3:15* with these exhortations*:* "But sanctify the Lord God in your hearts, and be <u>ready always to give an answer to every man that asketh you a reason of the hope that is in you</u>, with meekness and fear." (Emphasis added.)

Obviously, if a person quotes what they have heard, then it is an assumed belief. If this person is asked why they believe a certain way, and responds by referring to a source other than personal conviction established by the Word of God and confirmed by Holy Spirit, then it is obviously presumption on the part of the person. Such a presumption simply reveals that the person who is assuming that a matter is right is operating from the premise of blind hope.

In blind hope, this individual will simply hide behind this presumption to relieve self of being responsible for establishing and maintaining a right foundation. However, the Word of God is clear. The truths of God are simple enough for a child to embrace by faith *(Matthew 18:1-4; 2 Corinthians 11:3)*. Therefore, each of us as believers are able and capable of giving an answer for what

---

[25] The various meaning of words in this study came from two sources: Strong's Exhaustive Concordance of the Bible and the Webster's New Collegiate Dictionary.

we see as our hope in regard to all spiritual matters. *Colossians 1:27* clearly reveals what constitutes the hope within each believer, it is Christ in us, the hope of glory.

How can people know how much of their foundation is made up of presumptions and assumptions? By knowing this answer, struggling souls can put their beliefs in the right perspective. In other words, if people's foundation is full of presumptions and assumptions, they must hold lightly to what they believe, and give God permission to shake up their foundation.

Shaking foundations will allow individuals to test their personal beliefs with the Word of God to see how well they withstand the shaking. However, such a thought is frightening for most people. After all, what if He shakes everything and nothing is left standing on their foundation? They would have to once again start establishing a new foundation.

It is important to understand what is at risk for these people. They have given their heart, time, resources and energy for what they perceived to be truth. To many of them they have a hard time considering that their religious experiences were a waste of time. They would like to think that there is something that could be salvaged in the devastation of it all. Sadly, what many of these individuals discover is that even those things that have a semblance of truth have been tainted in some way by the poison of heresy.

The battle for these people to simply embrace truth can be intense. It takes everything in them to focus their confusing mind and conflicting heart on one goal, and that is to know the truth no matter what. After all, it will be the uncompromised truth that sets them free from the oppression, hurts, and wounds that have been left in their souls by those who have betrayed their trust *(John 8:32)*. At such times they must remember that many times those who betrayed them were deceived as well and had no ill intention towards them.

The Bible also brings the contrast as to the urgency for each believer to not just know the truth, but to love it. It warns about the impending destruction to those who do not love the truth. They will be turned over to delusion *(2 Thessalonians 2:10-12).*

In light of this warning, each believer must individually choose the truth in spite of what it might reveal about their foundation. Obviously, the only one who can reveal the stability of our foundation is God. It is at this time that we each need to examine our personal foundations. Based on the percentage of 1-100%, ask God how much of your foundation is actually made up of presumptions and assumptions.

The Premise of Truth

How concerned should we be if presumptions and assumptions make up over 50% of our foundation? In other words, we cannot give a scriptural answer from the premise of personal conviction and knowledge for 50% or more for what we consider to be our beliefs. Keep in mind, these beliefs may well determine our eternal destination. Therefore, we could be in serious trouble. However, let us say that 20%-40% of our foundation is made up of presumptions and assumptions. In this figure, we are assured of being over 50% right, but is such a percentage good enough when it comes to truth? To understand the seriousness of being even one percent off truth, we first must come to terms with how truth operates in our lives.

It is important at this time to consider that presumptions and assumptions often represent areas of indoctrination. The Bible is clear that we need to be guided into all truth by the Holy Spirit *(John 16:13).* However, many people associated with religion are not guided; rather, they are indoctrinated by their religious leaders or systems. On a separate sheet of paper for your personal edification, be ready to answer the questions presented in this study. The first question is what is the difference between indoctrination in and guidance towards the truth?

Here is a statement that we need to get into our spirits. "People are never indoctrinated into truth; rather, they are indoctrinated into man's point of view about a matter." The way people perceive will determine how they will interpret the truth. However, truth does not have to be interpreted; instead, it has to be recognized and believed as being truth. Therefore, indoctrination involves imbuing a particular opinion, point of view, or principle.

In Christianity, such indoctrination often points to an emphasis of certain doctrines or spiritual beliefs as being the truth, rather than the person and life of Jesus. Needless to say, such doctrines can have a personal twist or distortion to them that can oppose truth, rather than adhere to it *(2 Peter 2:1-3; 3:16).*

It is not unusual that doctrine, which finds it origins in indoctrination, to be inundated with Scripture, but when you compare Scripture with Scripture and test the intent or spirit behind it, such doctrine becomes unscriptural. In fact, all one needs to do to change the spirit or intent of God's truth is to change the meaning or emphasis behind a word.

For example, take the word meekness. "Meekness" means controlled strength or rage. However, if you take the meaning that is often associated with this word in our culture and apply it to Jesus in His humanity, the definition of Him would be a wimp, rather than one whose very strength and being was under the control of the Holy Spirit.

This brings us to the importance of emphasis. Religious leaders can emphasize good Scriptural points, but still miss the intent of the whole counsel of God's Word. For example, they can emphasize holiness, God's love, grace, works, repentance, sovereignty, etc., but the truth of God's intention and purpose is still absent. These leaders may also have what appears to be the right emphasis, but with the wrong presentation or approach because they are in a wrong spirit, promoting their own personal religious agenda.

The problem with starting from a wrong or biased presentation is that people will end up defining the perspective as to how they look at it according to the spirit that is influencing them. In other words, the particular emphasis will serve as a main theme or point through which all matters will automatically be viewed. It is the same concept as looking through rose-colored glasses. Everything will appear rosy, but in reality, it is a false presentation.

For cult members to understand how they are defining religious matters, they must consider what their religious leaders emphasized the most in their different religious presentations. Obviously, it would do each of us well to consider the type of emphasis we are exposing ourselves to when it comes to the religious influences in our lives.

How does each of us consider whether the religious theme being purported is correct? Here are some questions to consider. Does it allow God to be God? For example, some themes exalt one aspect of God such as His love, especially in a worldly fashion, while ignoring or downplaying another attribute of God such as holiness. Does it present a balanced picture of God's work and intervention on behalf of man? For instance, an important theme of the Bible is salvation. Clearly, we see where God saves because of His grace, but in some religious circles, it is taught that man's works are a necessary ingredient in order to obtain salvation. In this case, God's grace is being frustrated or made void by the attempts of people who strive to become righteous by their own merits. The fruit of such emphasis are obvious because when challenged, people become vague or confused about God and His salvation *(Galatians 2:21; Ephesians 2:8-10).*

Is there one theme in the Bible that allows for God to be God, presents a balanced picture of His works and ways, and brings the proper contrast as to man's part in salvation, such as faith? The answer is yes. See if you can distinguish this theme by considering the following Scriptures: *Romans 5:10; 2 Corinthians 5:18-19; Ephesians 2:14-18;* and *Colossians 1:20-23.*

God's heart is to establish a relationship with each of us that will promote spiritual growth, joy, peace, and satisfaction. It is a relationship where we will be able to enjoy Him, and He is able to enjoy us. This relationship has many aspects to it, but ultimately it will satisfy all desires of the heart, bring unspeakable joy to the soul, peace to one's being, and produce a hope that will never waver in light of eternity.

By changing the intent of something, you can actually redefine the character and work of God along with His many other truths. Clearly, man is vulnerable to influences and persuasions that could cause him to deviate from the truth, and embrace a lie, even when Scriptures are improperly used as a disguise to confirm or verify a matter.

In trying to understand the diligence of the Bereans in *Acts 17:10-12,* it is important to realize that they were comparing scripture with scripture to see if the Apostle Paul's teaching was in line with the intent of the full counsel of God's Word. This comparison was to ensure the integrity of God's Word. However, most indoctrination has to do with how man perceives or interprets the Word. It is important to point out that truth always stands on its own, but Scripture does not. One must always compare Scripture with Scripture to ensure a correct perspective.

Again, it is not unusual for people to use Scriptures to validate their wrong perceptions, but the Scriptures they use are taken out of context to form a biased picture or belief system. In fact, indoctrination of people by using certain phrases or words, along with specific terminology can cause them to close themselves off to any challenge that might set them free to test their foundation and explore God's truth beyond their established comfort zones of indoctrination.

Indoctrination of this type is destructive at any level. Undoubtedly, some of the religious leaders of Jesus' day were indoctrinating people by teaching their own traditions. Jesus told them that they made the Word of God ineffective, and their worship a useless exercise *(Matthew 15:3-9)*. He also made this statement, *"But woe unto you, scribes and Pharisees, hypocrites! For ye shut up the kingdom of heaven against men; for ye neither go in yourselves, neither suffer them that are entering to go in"* (Matthew 23:13).

Indoctrination closes down a person's ability to discern. It has only one goal and that is to influence and control how a person thinks. On the other hand, God wants to transform our way of thinking. For the sake of avoiding assumptions about this matter, we each need to know the difference between influence and transformation. The answer to this matter can be found in the different meanings of these two words, as well as in *Romans 12:1-2.*

Even if indoctrination has scriptural merit, it still erects a perspective that will only allow people to interpret the Bible according to what they have been systematically taught. It does not encourage the recipients to test such matters, which requires them to think outside of the box.

Thinking outside of their indoctrinated understanding produces confusions and fear. Since indoctrination is influenced by a wrong spirit, those who are held captive by their indoctrination will be prevented from seeing the truth, or when challenged by truth, will quickly become closed to it, rejecting it as a lie.

It is also important to acknowledge two important facts. The first fact is that all of us have been exposed to indoctrination in some way. The second fact we must acknowledge is that we can always find people and teachings to confirm any desired belief, regardless of whether it is truth or not. However, can any of us, as believers, afford to settle for any real interpretation of man in any area of our lives? Indoctrination closes people down to some extent from thinking outside of its presentation. We can clearly see this scenario in much of our public education.

We need to consider how much we have been indoctrinated to believe someone's interpretation of God, the Bible, and life by honestly grading our present belief systems in the following ways: (E) Extremely indoctrinated to the point that terms and words can close me down to any constructive challenge; (C) indoctrinated enough to cause confusion when challenged outside of the box; (M) possess a mixture of indoctrination and truth, but cannot really discern truth from indoctrination; (S) somewhat indoctrinated, causing vagueness in important spiritual foundational beliefs; (O) maintained open mind in spite of any indoctrination, but am struggling with what is true because of the past influence of man or a wrong spirit. (If unsure, ask the Lord to reveal the extent of your indoctrination.)

The question is how can believers know whether something is truth? All lies have a semblance of logic that can be adjusted and presented to appear as if they are truth to man's intellect. The Bible is clear that we can know the truth, but not all are receptive towards it. In some cases, people mishandle the truth, incurring the wrath of God upon themselves. The Bible is clear that we can do nothing against the truth, only for it *(Romans 1:18; 2 Corinthians 13:8). Proverbs 23:23* gives us this vivid instruction, *"Buy the truth, and sell it not; also wisdom, and instruction, and understanding."*

This brings us down to the premise of truth. Truth is absolute and unchangeable. If people do not start from what is truth, they cannot expect to come out finding or knowing truth. A good example of a premise of truth is creation.

32

The first book of the Bible tells us that God created all that is visible. Therefore, it is from this premise that man must consider all creation. Granted, truth can be confused or discredited by unfounded implications, theories, and lies by those who hate it, but since it is consistent and unable to be refuted, all truths concerning creation fit nicely into the teaching of creationism. However, if you take the humanistic theory of evolution, it can only stand in a class of its own. It sounds logical because it stays away from certain facts and laws. Instead of coming from the center of truth, it has to start on the outside fringes of what is acceptable logic, and work its way towards the center by trying to explain away, ignore, and discredit that which is already established as truth.

Evolution can only be upheld in ignorance and maintained within its own perverted arena because it does not fit into the workings of creation. For example, the theory of evolution is not consistent with the Law of Thermodynamics, and discoveries such as DNA. These different laws and discoveries point to Intelligent Design, which clearly refute this humanistic theory.

Therefore, indoctrination unfairly establishes in people the premise in which all things will be judged. This, then, is a perverted view, as opposed to the truth, which serves as the premise by which all things must be considered, weighed, and tested.

Indoctrination will also cause people to close down to any challenge, while truth will embrace challenge because it will always be confirmed, especially to those who are truly seeking it. Indoctrination insists that the ignorance it is creating is light and not darkness. Truth, on the other hand, serves as the light, and has nothing to fear. Once again, you can do nothing against the truth, only for it. In the end, truth will stand, as all falsehood will crumble under judgment.

The necessary question is, is there one standard of truth that the searching soul can trust? *John 17:17* says, *"Sanctify them through thy truth; thy word is truth."*

Attitude Towards
The Word Of God

According to the *Gospel of John,* the Word of God serves as the absolute standard in which to test all matters. The most fundamental stand that Christians lay claim to is that the Bible is the only inspired and authoritative written Word of God. But the question is, how many approach the Bible as if it is the infallible Word of God? *2 Peter 1:19-21* states this case,

> *We have also a more sure word of prophecy, unto which ye do well that ye take heed, as unto a light that shineth in a dark place, until the day dawn, and the day star arise in your hearts; Knowing this first, that no prophecy of the scripture is of any private interpretation. For the prophecy came not in old time by the will of man, but holy men of God spake as they were moved by the Holy Ghost.*

Do religious people assume, or really believe, that all biblical prophecies are not of any private interpretation? Do they believe it is sure? On the other hand, is it one of those beliefs that they presume is truth, but in reality, they are unaware that they are denying it because of a wrong attitude towards the Word? After all, those who interpret the Word for us in preaching and teaching will often become the final authority as to what we believe. Answer the following question. (Yes, I believe it is not of any private interpretation, or no I do not believe it has not been inspired by the Holy Spirit.)

Notice that the word Peter used in his letter was the word "prophecy". The word "prophecy" means prediction. In other words, are the predictions of the Bible sure? This is important because to fulfill prophecy would require powerful intervention. Fulfilled prophecies serve as the means of proving that God is indeed capable of maintaining the integrity of His Word.

The integrity of the Word does not address the minor discrepancies that so many skeptics point to as a means to warrant their unbelief; rather, it is a matter of maintaining the intent or spirit of it. If you honestly consider the discrepancies found in the Word, they do not change the main themes of the Bible nor do they alter the character of God, His heart and commitment towards us, His ways concerning truth, and His works on our behalf.

Many prophecies have been fulfilled concerning Tyre, Petra, Nineveh, and Egypt, as well as those surrounding Israel. In fact, one man, when asked how he knew the Bible was true, answered with one word, "Israel."

God is not through with Israel, but the fulfilled prophecies concerning this nation are incredible. However, the prophecies that are the most compelling as to the surety of God's Word and power are those that surround Jesus Christ. In his book, *Evidence That Demands A Verdict*, Josh McDowell points out the probabilities of just eight prophecies being fulfilled according to the modern science of probabilities. The probability for eight prophecies to be fulfilled would be 1 in 100,000,000,000,000,000. To comprehend this, you would have to take this many silver dollars and spread them throughout the state of Texas. They would actually cover the state two feet deep. You would then mark one of these silver dollars and mix it up in the great mass of coins. Next, you would blindfold a man and ask him to somehow locate and pick up that marked coin. What chance would this man have in locating the marked coin? He would have the same chance that the prophets would have in writing just eight prophecies and having them fulfilled in one man. Yet, according to the book, *All the Messianic Prophecies of the Bible,* by Herbert Lockyer, Jesus fulfilled an estimated 300 prophecies.

Each fulfillment of prophecy makes the odds go higher, validating the integrity and validity of the Written Word. Based on prophecy, not the doctrine of man, the Written Word is sure because the author of it is true to His word, and more than able to bring it forth, while maintaining its integrity. In *Romans 3:4* and *Titus 1:2,* we are told that God doesn't lie and if there is any deviation from truth it will be found at the door of man.

If the attitude of people is wrong about the Bible, they will not believe it to be true. If they do not believe it to be true, then they will strip it of its power to affect their lives properly. Such an attitude will destroy the power the Word must have in their lives to set the record straight as far as personal beliefs.

This issue of truth proves to be a real struggle for those who are former cult members because God's Word was not only perverted, it has been stripped of its truth and power by making it subservient to the heretical beliefs that were established as foundational.

It is vital that as Christians we test our real attitude and approach towards the Bible. Former cult members remind me that Christians can take much for granted when it comes to their foundation. We can mentally presume we recognize the authority of the Word, but our attitude or approach towards it could reveal that we really do not regard it as a personal authority in relationship to our lives.

Consider the following Scripture, *"All scripture is given by inspiration of God, and is profitable for doctrine, for reproof, for correction, for instruction in righteousness" (2 Timothy 3:16).* (Emphasis added.) Does this Scripture say most of the Scriptures are given by inspiration; therefore, we can ignore some? If we can ignore or explain away some, the question remains which Scriptures will we discredit and which ones will we believe?

One of the signs of a cult is that it believes the Bible "as far as it is translated" in correlation to the belief system it maintains. If people are indoctrinated, they will automatically discredit those Scriptures that oppose their leader or denomination's point of view. As a result, personal attitudes need to be exposed towards the Word of God in order to see if a person's attitude is correct.

In order to properly challenge wrong attitudes, believers need to understand what *2 Timothy 3:16* should mean on a personal basis. At this point, the reader is encouraged to meditate upon and write a summary of what the Scripture in *2 Timothy* means to them.

Obviously, the complete Word of God is profitable in establishing right doctrine, to bring proper reproof in the area of error, possesses the authority to bring proper correction in areas of wrong attitudes and practices, and ultimately bring instruction in regard to true righteousness. The issue as to whether the Bible has this type of authority in one's life comes down to how they approach the Bible.

There are different ways in which people approach the Bible. Some approach it from a doctrinal point of view. In the end, such people will adjust the Word according to their doctrine, rather than test and adjust their doctrine to the Word of God.

Some approach it from an intellectual level. They want the facts to establish or confirm their present understanding about spiritual matters. As a result, they will only see what they want to see on an intellectual level, while ignoring the other facets of Scripture. In most cases, people approach the Word of God from a self-serving basis to confirm what they consider to be their present truth, but few approach the Bible to find what truth is according to the Word of God.

Romans 10:17 tells us how to approach the Word of God. We are to approach the Word with the intent to receive it as truth by faith. Faith begins where personal understanding ceases. Since personal understanding is not serving as the premise in which a person will view the Word, it will ensure the Word's integrity and powerful impact, while establishing itself as the authority in a person's life. (Also, consider *Romans 14:23; 2 Corinthians 5:7; 13:5; Ephesians 2:8-9;* and *Hebrews 11:6.*)

It is vital we understand what role the Word of God plays in our lives. First, we must consider how it relates to our spiritual growth. *(See 1 Peter 2:2; Hebrews 5:14.)* Milk points to the pure doctrine of the Word. The Scriptures in *Hebrews 5:13-6:2* bring this out. The writer of *Hebrews* exhorts Christians to graduate from the stage of milk to solid food or meat by leaving the principles of the doctrines of Christ, and going on to perfection or spiritual maturity.

The problem with keeping a person at the level of doctrine is that they will remain carnal or fleshly in their way of thinking. Since cults establish a false doctrine as a foundation under cult members, these former members cannot even graduate from milk to meat. Instead, they wrestle with the fact that the milk (doctrine) they did partake of was contaminated. In a way, they have to throw out all the milk in order to taste the pure milk of Christ's doctrine. Pure milk is required before a person can graduate from the stage of carnality to a place of being able to walk properly in the ways of righteousness.

The Corinthians were struggling with carnality *(1 Corinthians 3:1-11).* For these Christians, this carnality translated into schisms in the body of believers. Carnality causes man to look to man. For the Corinthians they placed their value in being associated with men rather than Jesus Christ. Clearly, carnality in a Christian causes inconsistency in their walk.

Another problem with keeping people at the milk level where they are dependent on doctrine and man, is that they never learn to discern. *Hebrews 15:12-13* brings this fact out.

Discerning is the ability to discern the spirit or intent of a matter to ensure righteousness. Righteousness is not just a matter of doing right, but of being right or having right standing before God. Right standing involves having a right spirit to ensure the integrity of attitudes, approaches, and actions. Such integrity will prevent people from mishandling the truth.

Truth, when it is properly maintained, will have the necessary impact or effect on the way people think and operate. Therefore, discerning is of the utmost importance when it comes to properly identifying the spirit that is operating, not only in others, but also within ourselves. Take a moment to consider *Proverbs 16:2, Hebrews 4:12* and *1 John 4:1* in light of discerning the spirit motivating you or that is operating in your present environment.

We do not have to debate as to why some leaders keep people at the milk or diaper stage of Christianity. These people want these poor souls to be ever learning according to their perspective, but never coming to the knowledge of the truth that will enable them to properly discern spirit and take authority over their own spiritual growth *(2 Timothy 3:7).*

Discernment points to the fact that the Word of God is a spiritual book. In other words, the deep truths (meat) of the Bible are only realized in the spiritual realm and not on a natural level. Consider what *1 Corinthians 2:10-14* says about this matter. Since the Bible is a spiritual book, only the Holy Spirit can properly discern how its truths must be applied to our lives.

Answer the following question: Why must the Word of God be approached from the perspective of right spirit in order to gain truth? *(See 1 Corinthians 2:5-14; 15:51; Ephesians 1:9; 3:3, 9; and Colossians 1:26; 2:3)*

The mysteries contained within the Word of God can be unveiled through revelation, realized in wisdom (that is neither of man nor of this world), and brought forth in knowledge tempered by virtue and self-control *(2 Peter 1:5-7).* In light of this information, do you think that mere man can unveil the depths of these truths to our spirits? *(See John 16:7-13 and 1 John 2:27.)*

The Holy Spirit is the One who leads us into all truth and teaches us the deep things of God. He is the One who inspired the Word and ensured its integrity through the ages. As a result, we as believers have the means to discern between what is good (acceptable) and what is evil (wicked) when it comes to all spiritual matters and practices.

As stated, there are a couple of major themes in the Bible, but one of those themes is that as believers we can, we should, and we must know God. It is from the premise of who God is and His work that all matters must be considered and weighed. The Bible serves as God's diary. We can see into His heart, know His will, hear His cries, and discern His call. The Bible never instructs us to seek doctrine or personal understanding and knowledge, but to seek God, and we will live *(Jeremiah 29:13; Amos 5:4-8)*.

The question is, has this study thus far changed your attitude and approach towards the Word of God? If so, in what way?

Section 2

IN SEARCH
OF GOD

WHO IS GOD?

Who is God? When you question former members of a cult about how they perceive God, they often present a confusing mixture that may have some truth in it, but it digresses into some abstract or vague notion about God. In most cases, He seems far away from these people's understanding.

As Christians who may encounter former cult members, we need to be able to address this issue clearly. If the Word is dedicated for the purpose of God's saints knowing Him, then as His people, we must make it our priority to seek Him in Scripture and prayer for the purpose of growing in the knowledge of His character and ways.

However, how can people know God? If He is whom the Bible says He is, He is beyond mere man's comprehension. Yet, it is clear, we as believers must know Him. The best way is to begin with our personal perception of God. Who is He to me? Who is He to you? Meditate upon this, and then answer the question for yourself.

As believers, can we afford to have a vague idea about God? Can we settle for a concept of God? It is easy to put God into a nice theological box, but in doing so we run the risk of stripping Him of His personality. To keep Him on an intellectual level, as some do, is to demote Him in His majesty. According to *Daniel 11:32b*, *"…but the people that do know their God shall be strong, and do exploits."*

Obviously, any power and authority we possess will hinge on how much we personally know our God. Due to the fact that there are many gods, the real great search for those seeking His truth is to come to terms with who the God of the Bible is. For your personal edification what can you scripturally learn about the different gods? *(Jeremiah 10:6-15; Romans 1:19-28; 1 Corinthians 8:4-5; 2 Corinthians 10:4-5)*

In contrast, what do the following Scriptures say about the God of the Bible? *(Genesis 1:1; Exodus 3:4-6, 14-16; 20:1-5; 34:5-7; Psalm 91:1-9; 92:15; 100:3; Isaiah 43:10-11; 44:6-7; 45:5-9, 14, 18, 21-22; 46:9; 48:12; 49:7; Lamentations 3:22-26; James 2:19)*

When we consider other gods, in most cases, we are talking about idolatry. The big difference between the God of the Bible and other gods is that the God of the Bible created the heavens and the earth, while man creates other gods according to the vain imaginations of his heart and mind. It is man that gives false gods their preeminence in his life by giving them identity, erecting them into a place of importance, and coming under their false authority *(Psalm 115:2-9; Isaiah 2:8; Ezekiel 8:7-12; 14:3-7)*.

The problem with idolatry is that it becomes an avenue in which the kingdom of Satan can work in its darkness, play on people's ignorance about God, and replace the true God with the worship of demonic entities. The harsh reality is that demons are behind all idolatry. In *1 Corinthians 8:4-6,* gods also point to magistrates or judges, while lords point to masters or owners.

Scripturally we know there is only one true God who deserves our worship because He is our Creator. In summation, He is the only One who deserves our consideration and service *(Psalms 81:9; Matthew 4:10; Luke 4:8; Colossians 2:18)*. It is important to realize that Satan, the god of this present world, is after our worship, and if he can get us to bow down to any idol, he has succeeded in undermining the authority of God in our lives and directing worship towards himself.

As our Creator, God stands distinct from all other gods. However, He also stands distinct as far as His identity from all other gods. How can we identify God? (See *Galatians 4:8.)* What does the word nature mean? "Nature" means the essence or attributes of something or someone that identifies or distinguishes them.

There is only one God by nature. He is not God because people refer to Him as God. He is God because of who He is. He is a being, entity, or person. What does it mean for God to be a being, entity or person?

The concept of "being" means that something does exist, while "entity" points to the existence of something as contrasted with its attributes. For example, demons are an entity. Such an entity's attributes identify and distinguish them as wicked. However, the concept of a "person" has to do with personality.

Personality serves as the means in which we can interact with another. Scripture stipulates that God is spirit, and in *John 5:37* we are told that no one has seen the shape, or form, of the Father *(John 4:24)*. However, we are also told God has manifested Himself in the man Christ Jesus *(1 Timothy 3:16)*.

Even though God is Spirit, He also has a distinct personality that enables others to interact with Him. He communed with Adam, walked with Noah, talked face-to-face with Moses, and met with Joshua. He could not interact with these men if He did not have a personality. We need to consider God according to the context of His person or personality.

In comparison, idols do not exist, except in the imaginations of those who worship them. Those who worship them give them an image, but they have no real personality in which to interact with them. In addition, any relationship with a demon is one sided, ending in grave oppression. Due to the interaction that God desires with us, Christianity is not a religion, but a relationship with the Living God. By understanding God's nature, we will have a sense as to how to properly respond to, as well as interact with Him in a relationship.

The Bible clearly identifies the attributes of God. Again, there is only one true God, and we can personally know Him. Some of

His attributes are that He is eternal, holy, faithful, merciful, and full of grace. These are just a few of God's traits. However, the one trait that stands out to me is that He is immutable or unchangeable in His nature, disposition, and ways *(Psalm 102:27; Malachi 3:6)*.

When you consider how life is constantly in a state of flux, we can begin to understand how important it is to us, as believers, that God is that immovable Rock. Winds of doctrine may come and go, but God never changes. Religion may change the face of God in the eyes of its followers through its different presentations of Him, but the God of the Bible remains the same. As a result, there should be no confusion about Him and His identity. However, confusion and problems always arise when man defines Him according to theology, doctrine, and personal agendas, instead of by the Spirit and truth of the Word of God.

The great confusion and debates surrounding the identity of the true God is the result of man refusing to simply believe the Bible about Him, and instituting his own understanding and conclusions into some doctrinal or theological presentation. Cults actually redefine or reimagine God. In the end, the beliefs, practices, or the leader becomes the latest god (idol) in a long line of idols that man exalts in his heart and mind. Eventually these false gods will be defeated and brought down. If they are re-erected, it is because of man's ignorance towards the real God.

Three aspects of God properly identify the one true God. These points of identification begin with the fact that He is our Creator (what He has done), and that He has a distinct nature (Who He is). The final aspect is what He deserves. Because of who He is and what He has done, He alone deserves our worship.

It is vital that we keep this presentation about God simple. After all, the Word of God can be overwhelming to those who do not possess a clear understanding about God. People become lost or take detours from the simplicity and truths of God's Word, causing them to lose their ability to properly discern or reason a matter out concerning their Creator. Let us now consider the God of the Bible.

The Father:

The Father is identified as God in *1 Corinthians 8:6*. Clearly, there is one entity known as God, the Father *(Ephesians 4:6)*. As stated, we can know the Person of the Father, due to the fact He has a personality in which we can interact with Him. Nevertheless, what do we need to understand about God being our Heavenly Father? Again, we must somehow bring a contrast as to what we assume we believe about God versus what the Word of God declares.

The first thing that the term "father" brings to mind is the type of relationship He desires with each of us: to be His children. That is simple enough, but who is our Father? What do we need to know and understand about Him to possess a personal sense of who He must be in our lives? What do the following Scriptures show us about God, the Father? *(Matthew 6:1, 4, 8, 14, 26, 32; 7:11; 16:17; Mark 14:36: Luke 6:36: 10:21-22; 12:30; John 5:37; 6:44, 65; Acts 1:4, 7; 2 Corinthians 1:2-3; Galatians 1:1, 3; Ephesians 1:17; Colossians 1:2; 2:2; 1 Thessalonians 1:1; 2 Thessalonians 1:1-2; James 1: 27: 1 John 3:1)*

In these Scriptures, we can learn some interesting facts about the Father. We know He is located in heaven, but how many of us understood until now that no man had really seen His shape, nor had the Jewish people heard His voice. This is interesting to me because people had actual encounters with God in the Old Testament such as Jacob, Moses, Joshua, and Isaiah *(Genesis 28:12-13; Exodus 3:2-6; 24:9-12; 33:9-11; 18-23; Joshua 5:13-15; Isaiah 6)* (Note, Joshua paid homage or worshipped the Captain of the LORD's host). Is there any discrepancy in Scripture concerning the Father? As previously stated, there are mysteries in the Bible. It is up to God to reveal them to us through His Spirit. The challenge is always there. Will each of us allow our logic to dictate to us, or will we choose to believe the Scriptures about the Father as true, and trust that in time the Holy Spirit will make sense out of them?

From these Scriptures, we know that the Father is after what is true and genuine. We also know that Jesus Christ was in total subjection to His will, and that He sent the promise of the Holy Spirit. He is the essence of love, displays mercy, desires to forgive, gives peace, hides spiritual mysteries from those who are prideful, reveals Jesus' identity, draws people to His Son, gives His people the spirit of wisdom and revelation, and He knows what we have need of and provides it. This makes Him Jehovah Jireh, our Provider. He knows the seasons concerning His eternal plan, raised up Jesus on the third day, and that He is part of the mystery concerning Jesus Christ.

1 Corinthians 8:6 calls the Father, God, and states, "of whom are all things." It is because of Him all things exist. This clearly shows us that the Father was involved with creation, which points to Him as the Designer of all things.

Without His design, nothing could or would exist. Being the designer of all creation also means that He fits the first criteria of being God in relationship to being our Creator. In *James 1:17*, it tells us that He is immutable or unchanging in His nature and ways, and in *John 4:23-24* we learn that the Father seeks those who will worship Him in spirit and truth. In fact, we are to give Him thanks in the name of Jesus *(Ephesians 5:20)*.

Philippians 4:20 summarizes it best, *"Now unto God and our Father be glory forever and ever, Amen."* As you can see, the Father fits all three criteria as far as being God.

Has your understanding of the Father changed or become enlarged? Obviously, we are only skimming the surface of who He is, for we know He is eternal. The question is, how do we, as believers, come to a greater understanding of the Father? He actually gives us a valuable key in coming to a greater awareness of who He is in *John 8:19, "Then said they unto him, Where is thy Father? Jesus answered, Ye neither know me, nor my Father; if ye had known me, ye should have known my Father also."*

Jesus stated that He is the way to the Father, the truth about the Father, and the place where life is established in the Father. He told His disciples that because they had known Him, they also knew the Father *(John 14:6-7)*. We see where there was confusion about this issue.

We then read these Scriptures in *John 14:8-9, "Philip saith unto him, Lord show us the Father, and it sufficeth us. Jesus saith unto him, Have I been so long time with you, and yet hast thou not known me, Philip? He that hath seen me hath seen the Father; and how sayest thou then, Show us the Father?"*

Obviously, to know the Father, we must come to terms with the Son.

The Son:

Who is Jesus Christ? How important is it for each of us to possess the understanding as to Jesus' real identity? Once again, former cult members will teach you the seriousness of this issue. As I have pointed out, if you could pinpoint the one Scriptural truth that is under attack when it comes to the majority of the cults, it comes down to Jesus' identity.

Most former cult members are people who have greatly struggled with the identity of the Son. Granted, these members may give a basic rundown about how Jesus is the Savior, but, the real difference does not rest in what Jesus did as far as the cross; rather, it comes down to **who He is**. This conflict has been great among the different theological camps. Is Jesus mere man or is He more? Is He simply a man who serves as a reflection of the Father in godliness and serves as a prophet in word and deed, or does He possess the very characteristics of the Father? If so, it would also mean that He possesses the very divine nature of God.

We could easily brush over this issue because we assume that we know what we believe about Jesus and presume that it is a matter that most Christians can agree with; but Jesus clearly warned believers of false Christ's in the end days. He made this statement in *Matthew 24:23-24, "Then if any man shall say unto you, Lo, here is Christ, or there; believe it not. For there shall arise false Christs, and false prophets, and shall show great signs and wonders, insomuch that, if it were possible, they shall deceive the very elect."*

The Apostle Paul made this statement: in *2 Corinthians 11:3-4,*

> *For I fear, lest by any means, as the serpent beguiled Eve through his subtilty, so your minds should be corrupted from the simplicity that is in Christ. For if he that cometh preacheth another Jesus, whom we have not preached, or if ye receive another spirit, which ye have not received, or another gospel, which ye have not accepted, ye might well bear with him.*

"Bear" in this text means to hold oneself up against. In other words, we need to challenge and bring contrast to one who preaches another Jesus.

The reason for this challenge can be found in *1 John 2:22-23, "Who is a liar but he that denieth that Jesus is the Christ? He is antichrist, that denieth the Father and the Son. Whosoever denieth the Son, the same hath not the Father; he that acknowledgeth the Son hath the Father also."* To believe another Christ implies that a person is under the antichrist spirit, and is rejecting the witness, claims, and reality of the Father. To believe or promote another Christ makes the individual a fraud.

Clearly, we must make sure that our understanding concerning the Son of God is right. The Apostle Paul stipulated that Jesus is the only real foundation upon which people must be established. If we have a wrong Jesus, we also fail to possess the Father. Such a prospect should cause us to tremble at the possibility that we have embraced another Jesus. For if we do not believe and possess the correct Jesus, we will not possess eternal life *(1 Corinthians 3:11; 1 John 5:12).*

At this point, we need to examine honestly the possibility that some, or even much of our understanding of Jesus may be traced back to man's presentation. We also must discern how much of our understanding is in line with the Word of God. This challenge will bring us to *Matthew 16:13-16.*

Jesus asked his disciples a very simple question in these Scriptures in *Matthew 16, "But who do men say that I, the Son of man, am?"* People's initial understanding of Jesus always comes from another person's presentation. As a result, we need to answer this question for ourselves.

Apparently, the popular belief of Jesus' day was that He was some great prophet like Elijah. Granted, Jesus was a prophet, but He was not Elijah or Jeremiah. Clearly, what the disciples heard from others was incorrect.

Jesus did not stop at the point of other people's personal take on Him. It is common to hear various contradictory witnesses about Jesus from others, making it easy for those who, because of ignorance, assumptions, or presumptions, choose to hide behind these opinions as they presume such presentations to be right. However, inevitably we are going to have to face what we personally believe about Jesus. We are personally responsible to know for ourselves who Jesus is. Jesus made this clear by His second question to Peter, *"But who say ye that I am?" (Matthew 16:15).*

If one follows the Scriptures, the answer becomes automatic, *"Thou art the Christ, the Son of the living God" (Matthew 16:16).*

What do these two different terms really mean? In many cases, these are well-known terms that are part of the Christian vocabulary, but they hold no real meaning for some in the religious realm.

It is generally accepted that Jesus is the Christ, but how many of us are operating from assumptions as to what it means for Jesus to be the Christ? For that matter, what does it mean for Jesus to be the Son of God? For an example as to what I am talking about, let us take the term "Christ".

"Christ" means the Anointed One of God or the Messiah. We know Jesus was anointed to carry out a specific mission *(Luke 4:18-19).* But what significance does the position of Messiah carry?

For the Jewish people the term pointed to the Promised One, the Son of David, the Son of man, and their future King who would deliver them. Remember, we need to consider the sure word of prophecy about the Messiah. After all, prophecy was the means used to identify Jesus. He had to fulfill all the prophecies about the Messiah so that He would be recognized as the Promised One.

In *Isaiah's* prophecy about the Messiah, we gain much insight into Him *(Isaiah 9:6-7).* First, He would be born a child and given as a Son. The government shall be upon His shoulders. Clearly, the Messiah would be born of woman, and He would be established as king. It is important to realize that a couple of the Gospels present Jesus from the premise of Him being the Messiah. *Matthew* shows Jesus as the King, while *Luke* shows Him as the Son of man who came to deliver His people. Both of these Gospels clearly trace Jesus back to King David.

From what premise does the Gospel of *Matthew* present the Messiah? Matthew tells us that the Messiah's earthly name shall be "Jesus" (Jehovah saves) and they shall call His name, "Immanuel," which is interpreted "God with us" *(Matthew 1:21-23).* The latter is a fulfillment of a prophecy found in *Isaiah 7:14.*

From what premise should we consider Jesus in *Luke*? Luke is also a fulfillment of *Isaiah 7:14*. Jesus would be born of a virgin. His name was to be "Jesus" and He would save His people. As you study Luke, you will realize this Gospel establishes a testimony as to Jesus' identity. However, Luke also establishes Jesus as the Son of the Highest or the Son of God *(Luke 1:21-32)*.

This brings us to the term "Son of God." Those who believe on Jesus are the children of God. Therefore, why is the Son of God unique? He is unique because Jesus was begotten by the Father.

Children of God are born into the kingdom of God, but Jesus was not born into the kingdom of heaven, He was begotten by the Father *(John 1:14; 3:3-5, 16)*. Since there are cults that see Jesus as simply a "man", as His followers we need to reason out the identity of Jesus by examining whether He was conceived by Mary through some physical encounter with the Father. Keep in mind, no man has seen the Father's shape. Therefore, He does not have a body, and since He is unseen, He must be worshipped in spirit and truth.

It is important we understand Jesus' origins. If He was conceived in a natural way, that would make Him a mere man. According to *Strong's Concordance,* "begotten" implies sole son. Jesus stated that He came from heaven, and that the Father had sent Him *(John 6:33, 38-40, 51, 57-58; 8:23, 29; 12:49; 16:28)*. How could Jesus be sent if He did not pre-exist? The main problem that cult members have concerning this matter is that some of them have been indoctrinated by their former cult to believe that Jesus was just a man; therefore, He did not come into existence until He was conceived and born.

As you study the different controversial beliefs claiming to be Christian, you will continually conclude that Jesus' identity is what often separates other beliefs from what is considered mainline Christianity. Almost all unaccepted beliefs rejected by mainline Christianity strip Jesus of His deity, and reduce Him to some type of created being. For example, such beliefs claim that He is a great prophet, an angel, the spiritual brother of Lucifer, a way-shower, a good man, etc.

This brings us to an important aspect that former cult members struggle over concerning this issue. Even though the Word of God can be used to challenge these controversial beliefs, cult members have been indoctrinated to present logical (although twisted) Scriptural arguments to defend their take on Jesus. For this reason, we as believers must be able to reason these matters out, not only for our personal sake, but also for those who are in bondage to heretical indoctrination.

In the past, I have had the opportunity to reason out Scriptural truths with those who have been indoctrinated by cult leaders. It not only allowed the light of Jesus' truth to shine through the darkness of confusion and betrayal, but it gave me a greater assurance about the foundation that God established by His Word and in my life.

For example, a former cult member discussed with me the confusion he had concerning Jesus as God Incarnate. To quiet this man's confusion, I scripturally started from the premise of Jesus' pre-existence before He came by way of the manger. When such Scriptures as *John 1:30; 8:58,* and *17:5,* were given to verify Jesus' pre-existence, this man was quick to present the explanation that he had been given by his cult was that the Son was in the bosom of the Father *(John 1:18).*

When I heard this explanation by this former cult member, I asked him how he personally interpreted this Scripture. Did it mean that Jesus was a concept of the Father that He would bring forth in due time, or did it mean He existed, but had not yet been revealed as the Son in human form until God's eternal plan to redeem man was ready to be carried out? Upon his explanation of what it meant for Jesus to be in the bosom of the Father, I then referred him to *Luke 16:23*, pointing out that it was recorded that Lazarus was in the bosom of Abraham.

According to this former cult member's vague interpretation of *John 1:18*, Lazarus would have not really existed. He would have simply been a figment of the imagination or concept of the rich man, even though the man in hell could see him, and communicate with Abraham. Just for the record, the word "bosom," implies a bay.

It was also pointed out to this man that Jesus was ascribed as having similar references as God such as those found in *Revelation 1:11:* "I am Alpha and Omega, the first and the last." (Refer to *Isaiah 48:12.*) This man had been indoctrinated well because he had an explanation for that bit of reference. His explanation was that after Jesus ascended to heaven, He was given these titles of being the Alpha and Omega.

Upon this explanation, I then challenged him with *Hebrews 13:8:* "Jesus Christ, the same yesterday, and today, and forever." It was pointed out that according to this Scripture Jesus has never changed. Therefore, He always has been the Alpha and Omega. Then, I challenged the former cult member to consider all of *Revelation 1:8*: *"I am Alpha and Omega the beginning and the end saith the Lord, who is, and who was, and who is to come, the Almighty."* (Emphasis added.)

This Scripture is saying the same thing. Jesus has always been the beginning and the end, He will always be the Alpha and Omega, and that He is the Almighty, or all-powerful God. Since Jesus is immutable, He is clearly fitting one of the three criteria that identify Him as God.

As the former cult member was chewing on this information, he was challenged with *John 1:1*. Needless to say, he was not so willing to address this particular Scripture. However, he gave the explanation that he had been given by his former religious teachers. Note, this former cult member's explanation is quite popular among those who denounce Jesus as being both God and man. According to this man's explanation, this particular Scripture had been mistranslated when the Catholics were translating the canon. The former cult member was then asked to explain away *John 1:2-3* while comparing these Scriptures to *1 Corinthians 8:6; Colossians 1:15-17* and *Hebrews 1:2-3*.

These Scriptures reveal Jesus as Creator, meeting the second criterion that clearly identifies Him as being God. Here is the summation of these Scriptures. The Word (Jesus Christ), who was with God from the beginning and who is God, created the world. He also upholds all things by the word of His power. The Apostle Paul tells us that by Jesus all things exist. The Father may have designed all of creation, but Jesus is the One who created everything that we see.

Consider *Titus 2:13, "Looking for that blessed hope, and the glorious appearing of the great God and our Saviour Jesus Christ."* Jesus is the one coming back and in this Scripture, He is referred to as the great God and Savior.

Why is it so important to come to terms with Jesus' origins? As we are about to see, in light of the term "Son of God" we will have to conclude that premise is everything if we are going to properly handle the Word of God.

For example, if Jesus is simply a man, how can He be the Son of God? If we properly understand the Scriptures, as well as the meaning of nature, Jesus can only be the Son of God if He possesses the nature of God.

For example, children inherit the traits of their parents. Being the sole Son of God implies that Jesus possesses the same traits as His Father. He declared that He was in the Father, and the Father was in Him *(John 14:10)*. Remember, it is recorded that the Father sent Jesus, but there are no claims that Jesus is a literal descendant or seed of the Father as He was of the woman, Mary.

Clearly, the Father is divine in nature, making that which is of Him, divine in nature as well. The word "of" means origins or derivation. Jesus came from the Father in the position of a Son. As man, Jesus found His source in the Father, but as the Son of God, His deity is clearly established and shows the type of relationship that in His humanity, He had with the Father.

In the beginning, Jesus was not known as the Son, but as the Word, the verbal and visible expression of God in nature and character *(John 1:1)*. According to one article I read, the term "the Word" refers to Yeshua, the One who embodies the Word of God. *John 1:14* tells us the Word became flesh. Jesus actually took on humanity.

As we consider this revelation of Jesus, *John 1:1* is the only premise by which we can understand Jesus as the Son of God. If this premise is removed, we are left with terms that have no meaning. Terms without meaning leave us with nothing that is substantial or trustworthy in which to test our beliefs about the Jesus of the Bible.

The key is, the Jewish people understood that the term "Son of God" meant Jesus was God. As you study their reaction toward Jesus being called or considered the Son of God, they thought it to be blasphemy and picked up stones to execute judgment on Him. *John 5:18* gives us this insight, *"Therefore, the Jews sought the more to kill him, because he not only had broken the Sabbath, but said also that God was his Father, making himself equal with God."*

"Equal" means to be the same as in nature, position, and importance. Does Jesus have the right to make such claims? The Apostle Paul made this statement in *Philippians 2:6, "Who, being in the form of God, thought it not robbery to be equal with God."* According to the "Strong's Concordance", the word "form" in this text means nature.

Jesus, who possesses the nature of God, did not think it was robbery when He ceased to be equal with God. What does this mean? When Jesus became man, He emptied Himself (became of no reputation), of His power and authority as God, took on the form of a servant, and was fashioned as a man, thereby, making Him lower than His very creation, the angels *(Philippians 2:7; Hebrews 2:9-11).* Jesus never ceased to be God, but His deity was clothed in humanity. The Apostle Paul confirmed this when he stated that in Christ was the fullness of deity in bodily form *(Colossians 2:9)* It was upon the Mount of Transfiguration that His humanity was parted to reveal His true glory as God *(Matthew 17:1-9).*

Matthew 28:18 tells us that the authority and power He relinquished as God to become man was given back to Him in His humanity. However, this authority would be channeled in a different way, leaving us an important example.

Jesus came under the authority of the Father, making His power subject to the Father's will and plan. We get insight into this very fact in *Matthew 26:51-56* and *John 10:18.* Jesus declared that no man could take His life, but He would lay it down as well as raise it again. On the night that He was betrayed He told His disciples He had the authority to request a legion of angels, but He was in subjection to the plan of the Father to fulfill His promise of redemption. In compliance with Jesus' example as man, it is obvious we must receive power from above to carry out our calling as well.

This brings us to the premise in which the Gospel of Mark presented Jesus in *Mark 1:1, "The beginning of the gospel of Jesus Christ, the Son of God."* Mark presents Him as the Son of God. However, there are other entities that recognized Jesus as the Son of God: the demons *(Luke 8:26-29).*

Consider the actions and words of one of the devils He encountered, *"Saying, Let us alone! What have we to do with thee, thou Jesus of Nazareth? Art thou come to destroy us? I know thee, who thou art, the Holy One of God" (Mark 1:24).* There are three points that need to be considered in this Scripture. 1) This demon was trembling before Jesus. The Word clearly tells us there is only one being that demons tremble before, *"Thou believest that there is one God; thou doest well. The devils also believe, and tremble" (James 2:19).* 2) This demon recognized that Jesus had authority over him. It is important to note Jesus did not stand in the authority, name, or power of His Father as we stand in Jesus' authority, name, and power. This brings us to the reason the demon had to give way to Jesus.

As Creator, Jesus has pre-eminence over all thrones, dominions, principalities, and powers (*Colossians 1:15-18*). 3) The final aspect of this Scripture is that the demon referred to Him as the Holy One of God. As you study the concept of holiness, there is only One who is ascribed as being Holy—that is God *(Isaiah 6:3; Matthew 19:16-17)*.

There are also other Scriptures where Jesus is actually referred to as God. In *1 Timothy 1:17* Jesus is called the King eternal and the only wise <u>God</u>. This statement is made about Him in *1 Timothy 3:16, "And without controversy great is the mystery of godliness: God was manifest in the flesh, justified in the Spirit, seen of angels, preached unto the nations, believe on in the world, received up into glory."* Paul is pointing out that the mystery that had been hidden is that God would manifest Himself in the flesh. "Manifest" means to make apparent.

God had clearly made Himself apparent in human form. We also can read where Thomas called Jesus God in *John 20:28* and the Father even addressed Jesus as God in *Hebrews 1:6-8*.

Ultimately, Jesus was crucified because He was the Son of God. In an indirect way He admitted to the Pharisees that He was the Son of God, sealing His death on the cross *(Matthew 26:63-66)*. Yet, all that Jesus experienced was a fulfillment of Scripture to verify His identity and words.

Let me challenge you once again. How important is it to get the Son of God right? The Apostle John put forth this warning,

> *By this know ye the Spirit of God: every spirit that confesseth that <u>Jesus Christ is come in the flesh is of</u>*

God; And every spirit that confesseth not that Jesus Christ is come in the flesh is not of God; and this is that spirit of antichrist, of which ye have heard that it should come, and even now already is in the world (1 John 4:2-3). (Emphasis added.)

What is the Apostle John talking about? We already know that Jesus came into the world as man. There would be no debate about this matter, unless John was presenting this in light of *John 1:1.* In this case, it would mean that unless a person confesses that Jesus Christ, who is God by nature, actually came in the flesh, they are under an antichrist spirit. "Antichrist spirit" points to a spirit who will counterfeit or become a substitute for the real Jesus.

This brings us to another important aspect of Jesus as the Messiah. *Isaiah 9:6* says about the character and work of the Messiah "...and his name shall be called Wonderful, Counselor, The Mighty God, The Everlasting Father, the Prince of Peace." (Emphasis added.) The Messiah is also referred to as The Mighty God and the Everlasting Father. We must not forget the other name that refers to Jesus: "Immanuel," which means God with us *(Isaiah 7:14; Matthew 1:23).* In order to have a proper understanding of the Messiah, we must also consider Jesus Christ, the Anointed One of God in light of His deity.

The prospect of the Messiah being God brings us to a very important aspect of how the Jews handled this concept. They were clearly challenged with it in different ways.

We see one of these challenges concerning King David in *Matthew 22:41-46.* Jesus was considered and referred to as the Son of David, a term pointing to the Messiah. Jesus asked the Pharisees, *"What think ye of Christ? Whose son is he?"* They answered by saying that He would be the son of David. Jesus then asked them how could David in the Spirit call him Lord if the Christ was only his son?

59

This is an important question. Jesus took this reference from *Psalm 110:1*. This *Psalm* has Jehovah (LORD, God) telling David's Lord, (Jesus) to sit on His right hand until His enemies were made His footstool. You have to realize that as a committed Jew, King David would only recognize one to be His Lord—God *(Isaiah 43:11; 45:5, 21).* If you would like to study more about David's Lord, you can refer to *Isaiah 6*, where the prophet encountered Him. Note the spelling of Lord in *Isaiah 6:1-11* as compared to the spelling of it in *Isaiah 6:12.*

Consider both Scriptures in light of *Philippians 2:9-11.* Are you getting the impression that there are great mysteries in the Word of God beyond mere man's comprehension, especially about Him, and because of our finite status as man we can only know in part? This is why we must approach the Bible to believe it, and not approach it based on personal understanding or intellectual deduction.

There is also another confrontation in *John 8:48-59* with the Jews. Jesus told them if a person would keep His sayings, they should not see death. The Jews took issue with His statement. They declared that He had a demon for those who were righteous such as Abraham and the prophets were dead. These great men could not even give life, nor did they escape death. Then, they asked Jesus if He was greater than Abraham and the prophets. They ended with this challenge *"Whom makest thou thyself?"*

This important question must be reasoned out. Jesus was claiming to be greater than the great men of faith, and He also claimed that He could give life. This put Him in a different league than what they expected, even from the perspective of Him being the Messiah. Jesus assured them He knew the Father who they claimed they knew. If He acted as if He did not know the Father, He would be a liar. He told them that Abraham rejoiced to see His day, and he saw it and was glad. This was pointing to the incident where Abraham took Isaac to offer him as a burnt offering in *Genesis 22*, giving him a glimpse into God providing His Son as a sacrifice on our behalf. Jesus ended His confrontation with the Jews with these words, *"Verily, verily, I say unto you, Before Abraham was, I am."*

The Jews' response was to stone Jesus. Jesus clearly stated He existed before Abraham. Their reaction was also possibly in relationship to how Moses was instructed to present God to the children of Israel when they asked who sent Him. The Lord told Moses to tell them that *I AM* has sent him unto them *(Exodus 3:14).*

The I AM was the One who gave the children of Israel their Law at Mount Sinai. Jesus was implying that He was the "I AM." This was considered blasphemy by the Jews, for clearly Jesus was claiming to be Jehovah, the great Lawgiver. Did these Jews forget the prophecy about the Messiah in *Genesis 49:10-12?*

It said of the Messiah that He would come from the tribe of Judah. It pointed out that He was the scepter and a lawgiver. (See also *Psalm 60:7.)* Scepter points to a rod that will bring forth correction as well as a ruler. *Isaiah 11:1* tells us that this rod will come out of Jesse (King David's father), and *James 4:12* tells us that there is only one lawgiver. This lawgiver is able to save or destroy us.

Even with all the prophecies about the Promised One, the Jews became confused with Jesus' true identity. It did not make sense to them even though they were given valuable insight into Him. In spite of the miracles they had seen, they refused to believe He was the Christ. Even though He had authority over Satan, they accused Him of being subject to Satan and his kingdom.

Sadly, the same arguments have raged over the last 20 centuries about Jesus. Yet, King David believed and acknowledged the reality of the Messiah, and Abraham looked for Him, saw its fulfillment and rejoiced over the day the Messiah would make His entrance into history. And, when you consider that even the angels desire to look into the fulfillment of these promises, you realize that we can only approach and receive these promises by faith *(1 Peter 1:11-12).*

The next question is why did Jesus have to come in the flesh? He came to be a substitute. There could be no remission (pardon) of sin without the shedding of blood. Calves and goats could not secure such a pardon *(Hebrews 9:11, 22, 10:17).* No man could offer any sacrifice that would satisfy the Law of God. Therefore, God provided the sacrifice, the Lamb of God. God took on flesh to become that Lamb to secure redemption for our souls, and to serve as the only means of reconciliation back to the Father. After talking about that fact that the sacrifices of bulls and goats could not take away sins, *Hebrews 10:5* makes this statement, "Wherefore when he cometh into the world (Jesus), he saith, Sacrifice and offering thou wouldest not (not sufficient to take away sin), but a body hast thou prepared me (to become the Lamb of God). As the Lamb of God, Jesus would take away the sin of the world *(John 1:29).* (My emphasis in parenthesis.)

If what we have discovered in Scripture is true, Jesus is fully God and fully man. In *2 Peter 1:4* we are told that we are given great and precious promises that by these we might be partakers of the divine nature. As you consider this Scripture, it is in reference to partaking of Jesus who is divine by nature.

The Word tells us that in His humanity Jesus forgave sin. Forgiveness in this text can only be ascribed to God. As man, He knew the thoughts of men. Once again, only God knows the inner thoughts of man *(1 Chronicles 28:9; Matthew 9:4; Luke 5:20-24; 6:8).* He commanded the elements of earth such as wind and water *(Luke 8:24-25).* We know that only the Creator has such power over the elements of this world. As Man in the courts of heaven, He now serves as both our mediator and High Priest *(1 Timothy 2:5).* Jesus also serves as our foundation and the cornerstone. If we fail to come to terms with whom He is to ensure a proper foundation, He will be redefined and replaced as a cornerstone with a different Jesus. He warned that He was the Stone, and that people would fall over Him and be broken, or He would grind them to powder in judgment *(Matthew 21:42-44; 1 Corinthians 3:11; Ephesians 2:19-22 1 Peter 2:6-8).*

It can become quite overwhelming for people to consider these different aspects of Jesus. This presentation merely scratches the surface. If Jesus is eternal, we will only understand in part. If His work is eternal, it will carry a depth too great to comprehend. This study could go on and on in regards to the revelations surrounding the Son of God. *Ephesians 2:7* reminds us, *"That in the ages to come he might show the exceeding riches of his grace in his kindness toward us through Christ Jesus."*

However, there is one final criterion that Jesus must meet to identify Him as God, and that is worship. Did Jesus receive worship? The answer is yes.

The wise men worshipped Him as a baby. Joseph and Mary, who knew the Law, would not tolerate such worship unless they recognized Jesus as their Messiah, the Son of the Highest *(Matthew 2:11).* The angels worshipped Jesus *(Hebrews 1:5-6).* As you study the Bible, angels never received worship, but they clearly honor and worship their Creator.

Last, but not least, people worshipped Jesus throughout the Gospels. Unlike Peter, Paul, and Barnabas who refused to receive worship in any form because they were mere men, Jesus openly received people's worship *(Matthew 8:2; 9:18; 14:33; 15:25: 18:26; 28:9, 17; Mark 5:6; John 9:38; Acts 9:25-26; 14:12-18).* We see Him being worshipped around the throne of God as they make this powerful declaration, *"Saying with a loud voice, Worthy is the Lamb that was slain to receive power, and riches, and wisdom, and strength, and honor, and glory, and blessing"* *(Revelation 5:12 refer to Revelation 4:8; 5:11-14).*

Is Jesus a mere man or is He God incarnate? The issue of Jesus' identity reminds me of the incident that took place in

Jesus' hometown, Nazareth *(Luke 4:16-30)*. Jesus had stood up in the synagogue and read the prophecy about the Messiah found in *Isaiah 61:1-2*. He told them that the prophecy was fulfilled that day. These people knew what Jesus was declaring about Himself.

Consider what they said, *"Is not this Joseph's son?" (Luke 4:22b)*. What were they saying about Jesus? How could He be the Messiah? We know Him as the son of Joseph; therefore, He is of man, and from man, thereby, making Him a mere man. These people reacted in total unbelief towards Jesus. As a result, Jesus declared that the prophecy was fulfilled in their ears, rather than in their lives. Jesus' challenge eventually stirred these people to wrath. They tried to throw Him over a cliff. However, He simply passed through their midst.

We must constantly come back to the correct premise if we are going to properly reason out truths outlined in Scripture. As believers, we have been given sure prophecies in the Old Testament about the Messiah. We have also been given proof of the Son of man's identity through His teachings and miracles. We have been given a record or testimony of the Son of God that is clearly outlined in the New Testament. If we say He is merely a man, how much of the Word of God must we disregard, ignore, or explain away? If He is God Incarnate, can we conclude that all Scriptures concerning Him will fall into line with the full counsel of God's Word? After all, we can do nothing against the truth, only for it *(2 Corinthians 13:8)*.

The Apostle John warns us that if we do not believe the record we have been given concerning Jesus Christ, we will not possess eternal life *(1 John 5:9-13)*. If we fail to believe the record that has been given to us concerning the identity of Jesus, we can never be assured of eternal life. If we walk in unbelief towards the Jesus of the Bible, He will pass through our midst, without touching our lives with His salvation or deliverance.

The question remains the same. When you and I stand before Jesus as our Judge (*John 5:22*), and He asks that question which still rings down through the corridors of time, *"Who do you say I am?"* What will your answer be? What will my answer be?

The Holy Spirit

Who is the Holy Spirit? Most Christians have some notion, sentiment, or idea about the Spirit of God, but what do each of us really understand about Him? Is He a concept, an ideal, or a point of theology? In some religious arenas He is ignored altogether, while in others He is improperly emphasized and accredited with activity that is void of His power and fruit,

In the places where the Holy Spirit is improperly sought and overemphasized, it is not unusual to witness manifestations that are accredited to the Holy Spirit, but the fruit of the results leave people in confusion and feeling let down. Therefore, how important is it for believers to know the Holy Spirit?

1 John 4:1 tells us we must test the spirit behind all matters. But what is spirit? How do the saints test the spirit? Before this question can be answered, people must first come to terms with how they perceive the Holy Spirit.

Spirit comes down to what motivates a person. Motivation will determine the real intentions, causing people to focus on what is intended. The way to know what spirit is in operation is to consider what the real focus or emphasis is of the person. Christians can know people's spirit or intention by what they emphasize.

Although self-serving intentions may be covered up with religious terms and activities, they will eventually be exposed by what becomes these individuals' focus in a matter. The most popular emphasis for most cults is works that often manifests itself in service to the leaders.

Most of the emphasis on works in these cults are in relationship to the leadership, or in other words, serving the leadership's purpose and goal in building their personal kingdom. Therefore, what does this focus say about the motivation of such leadership? It pretty well says that it is self-serving. It also says something else. It is idolatrous.

After all, if something is not about glorifying or honoring the real God (the main purpose for all works), then it must be considered idolatrous. Idolatry is considered one of the works of the flesh, and those who walk in such works will not inherit the kingdom of God *(Matthew 5:16; Galatians 5:16-21)*.

The harsh reality is that the Holy Spirit is merely a vague notion to many Christians. For some believers, they are not sure who the Holy Spirit is. If they do not know who He is, how He works, and the part He plays in their lives, then how can they expect to test or discern what spirit is in operation.

Is the Holy Spirit a force (for He is unseen and works in the spiritual realm), an extension of God (for His origins and source are found in God) or a Person (someone who has a personality that we can interact with). Is the Holy Spirit an extension of the Father and Jesus? (Refer to *Galatians 4:6-; Philippians 1:19; 1 Peter 1:11)*. As you can see, the possibility of confusion can clearly exist about this subject.

Another area that causes confusion is the taboo that can be put on using the term "Holy Ghost. The Bible uses both terms, but there are those who are told not to use the term "Holy Ghost" because there has been some type of superstition attached to it. "Ghost" has the same meaning as "spirit." In fact, in the *Strong's Concordance*, "ghost" and "spirit" have the same reference number in the New Testament (#4151). It also must be noted that spirit points to soul, mind, or mental disposition, which brings us back to motivation, intention, and focus.

Emphasizing one term over the other reveals ignorance on people's part, not wisdom. Both terms are Scriptural and both mean the same thing. Granted, different terms may conjure up different images, but people's perception of a subject should not be based on personal images, but on the Word of God.

How does the Word of God present the Holy Spirit? Does it present Him as a force from God that simply moves upon people? "Force" means strength or energy exerted to bring forth a matter. Such energy has the ability to compel, constrain, or force to overcome any type of resistance. In some arenas "force" points to the New Age concept of good overcoming evil or light overcoming darkness. (See *Daniel 11:37-38* for a contrast. Note, our God is not a God of forces, rather He is a God that has power over all of Creation.) Does the concept of force or energy sound like a characteristic of the Holy Spirit? As we will see, He is a person; therefore, He is not a mere force. The Holy Spirit is not aggressive; therefore, He can be resisted. In fact, He will not always strive (contend or plea the cause) with man *(Genesis 6:3)*.

Now we come to the second possibility. Is the Spirit an extension of Jesus? There can be a couple of problems with this. First, if Jesus is mere man, how could His Spirit be in operation in the Old Testament without His existence *(Genesis 6:3; 2 Chronicles 15:1-2; 20:14)*? Obviously, for the Spirit to be in existence in the Old Testament, it seems that Jesus would have to be in existence as well.

Another problem is that the Spirit has no real distinction and that He is merely associated with God. If God has His own Spirit and Jesus His, this would contradict *Ephesians 4:4* that there is only one Holy Spirit. Of course, this could be possibly explained by the fact that God's Spirit is the same as the Spirit of Christ.

This brings us to the next possibility—that the Holy Spirit is a separate Person who acts distinctively in His duties, but is in submission to the Father's will and in alliance with the Son's mission. Remember personality implies the ability to interact with people. Personality denotes the person of someone. Does the

Spirit fit this criterion? Consider the fact that the Holy Spirit is referred to as "he" or "him" in Scripture *(John 14:27; 16:7, 13)*. "He" and "him" is a pronoun that is associated to a distinct person, not to a force or extension of something or someone.

It is interesting to note that the Spirit is used in conjunction with Jesus in *1 Corinthians 6:11.* If the Holy Spirit was an extension of Jesus, why did He have to come down and anoint Jesus after His baptism *(Matthew 3:16-17* refer to *Luke 4:18-19)?* If the Holy Spirit was simply an extension of the Father, why did Jesus have to go away before the Spirit could be sent by both Jesus and the Father *(John 14:26; 15:26; 16:7)?*

When Jesus was with His disciples, He could simply have extended the Spirit to them if the Spirit was an extension of Him. If the Spirit was an extension of the Father, why is it that He acts as a separate Person in His reactions to a matter? For example, He departed from Saul. *(1 Samuel 16:14). Romans 8:27* also makes reference to the mind of the Spirit, also implying that He is a distinct Person from the Father and the Son.

Does the Holy Spirit have a personality that can be observed in Scripture? We are told that He can be lied to, vexed, tempted, grieved, or quenched *(Isaiah 63:10; Acts 5:3, 9; Ephesians 4:30; 1 Thessalonians 5:19).* The Word of God tells us He spoke to men in both the Old and New Testaments *(2 Chronicles 20:14-15; Acts 8:29; 10:19). John 16:13* refers to Him as the Spirit of truth.

He is the one who leads each of us into all truth about Jesus, and teaches us all things concerning God. He is the Spirit of wisdom, understanding, counsel, might, and knowledge who ultimately reveals mysteries to and through men *(Isaiah 11:2; John 14:26* (refer to *1 John 2:27); 16:13; 1 Corinthians 14:2).* He is the One who brings to remembrance spiritual truths, and will connect the truths with God's real intent about a matter, bringing forth revelation *(John 14:26; Ephesians 3:3-5).*

Scripture definitely points to the Holy Spirit being a distinct person from the Father and the Son, but is He simply a spirit or is there more to Him? *John 4:24* tells us God is a Spirit. The Apostle Paul talked about the Lord being that Spirit in *2 Corinthians 3:17*. "Lord" in this text points to supreme in authority as in God, Lord, or master.

One of the most interesting Scriptures can be found *in Isaiah 48:16*: *"Come near unto me, hear this: I have not spoken in secret from the beginning; from the time that it was, there am I; and now the Lord GOD, and his Spirit, hath sent me."* This is in reference to the Messiah.

Remember John said that Jesus was the Word in the beginning. In this Scripture in *Isaiah*, the Promised One is declaring that what He spoke from the beginning is not a secret. Clearly, there is a reference to three distinct persons in this Scripture verse. However, note the Lord GOD and his Spirit sent the Messiah. The word "and" points to conjunction with. It implies the equality of both the Lord GOD and the Spirit in sending forth the Messiah. It is also important to note that the Son had to ascend to the Father before the Holy Spirit could be sent.

Do such references point to the Holy Spirit being God? We know that He is of God, but does He fit the criteria of God? How about creation? *Genesis 1:2* tells us: *"And the earth was without form, and void; and darkness was upon the face of the deep. And the Spirit of God moved upon the face of the waters."*

"Form" in this text implies an empty place or waste. "Void" means to be empty or undistinguishable. Jesus may have created everything, but it is the Spirit of God that recreated the face of the world, and garnished the heavens *(Job 26:13; Psalms 104:30)*. He is the One who brought life, order, beauty, and purpose to the world and heavens. *Job 33:4* states that the Spirit of God made man, and that the breath of the Almighty has given life. In summation, the Holy Spirit was the breath of life that was given to Adam in *Genesis 2:7* that distinctively set him apart as a living soul.

The work of recreation and order is consistent with the Spirit's work in the believer and in the Body. For the believer, they are born again with the Spirit and with Water (the Word) *(John 3:3, 5,* refer to *Ephesians 5:26* and *1 Peter 1:23* in regards to the Word; *Galatians 4:29).* The Holy Spirit is the breath of life that comes into a new convert, making the believer a new creation by reviving and renewing the spirit of their inner being with new life, as well as transforming their mind *(Romans 12:1-2; 2 Corinthians 4:16; Ephesians 4:23).*

The Holy Spirit is the one who actually establishes the disposition and life of Christ in the believer *(2 Corinthians 3:6, 17-18).* He is also the One who baptizes and places each believer into the Body of Christ, and gives them gifts for the purpose of edification for the whole Body *(1 Corinthians 12:7-13).* Note, that the Spirit gives these gifts as **HE WILLS**, pointing to the fact that He is sovereign in His work *(1 Corinthians 12:11).*

Does the Holy Spirit possess the attributes of God? We know He is completely holy due to His identification as the Holy Spirit, but He is also eternal *(Hebrews 9:14).* However, can we find in Scripture where He is immutable? Even though He is of God and from God who is unchangeable, it is important to test out this vital characteristic because the Holy Spirit will prove to be consistent in character and manifestation.

The Word of God bears out the consistency of the Holy Spirit's character and work. The Spirit of God has always manifested Himself in gifts in both the Old and New Testament. When He came down upon men in the Old Testament, they prophesied, and when He moves among the New Testament Church, gifts such as prophecy are a manifestation *(1 Samuel 10:10-11; 19:20-24; Acts 2:1-17; 1 Corinthians 12:7, 10).* "Manifestation" in this text means expression or exhibition of the

Spirit, which is consistent with Him moving upon men to bring forth the sure prophecy of the Word of God *(2 Peter 1:19-21)*?

The Holy Spirit has never changed as to how He moves and manifests Himself. He has moved in the midst of God's creation. He has always come upon man to bring insight and revelation to God's truths. We see this uniformity in both testaments, but there is one difference. In the Old Testament, the Holy Spirit would only come upon men and move upon them to speak forth the oracles of God, but now He not only comes upon men, but He abides within them through the born-again experience *(John 3:3, 5)*.

In fact, believers are known as the temples of the Holy Spirit. The Holy Spirit represents the very presence of God in the midst of His people. He not only moves upon, but He moves in and through man to bring forth the life of Christ in each believer *(1 Corinthians 3:16-17; 6:17-19)*. Since He resides in believers, He has access to move through the Body of believers to bring proper instruction, warning, and encouragement.

It is vital for believers to understand how the Holy Spirit expresses Himself. Remember as believers, we are to test the spirits. The reason we can test the spirits is that their fruits are tangible *(Matthew 7:16-20)*. These fruits can be properly discerned by considering the environment that is being established.

The Holy Spirit sets up the environment of righteousness that allows God to have His way. For example, the fruit of the Spirit represents the inward disposition or environment of man *(Galatians 5:22-23)*. Disposition will manifest itself in attitude and approach. If the Holy Spirit is present, a person will be motivated by love, will possess an anchor of abiding confidence due to joy, peace will reign because of a right relationship with God, and the person's attitude will reveal patience, kindness, and moral accountability. Such a person will approach all matters in faith, meekness, and temperance. The result of such an environment is that of order which is made evident by reconciliation with God *(1 Corinthians 14:33).*

People who operate outside of the Spirit will be plagued by uncertainty, chaos, and confusion. This is brought out in the Old Testament as you consider men such as Saul and David. In the New Testament, you can observe the order wrought by the Spirit of God being upheld in the Body. The Apostle Paul dealt with the attitude as well as the guidelines that the gifts of the Spirit are to operate within *(1 Corinthians 12; 14).* If the right attitude is missing and the guidelines disregarded, then one can easily conclude that there is a wrong spirit in operation.

This brings us to the subject of order. How does one come into order? The answer is that people must come back to center. The center is God. Therefore, the Holy Spirit will always lead people back to Jesus. When people end with any other sense of someone or something (other than Jesus), such as self (often expressed in emotional hype or impulsiveness), man's-leadership (false security and idolatry), or man-made religion (pious experience), they will quickly find themselves empty, uncertain, and frustrated.

Such people give the impression that they have to go back every week to get their regular religious "fix" in order to keep going. The only place where people can find lasting satisfaction is in Christ. Therefore, the Holy Spirit will always lead each of us back to our need, dependency, hope, and life in Jesus *(John 14:6, 26; 16:13-14).*

As Christians, we must also test the spirit that is not only operating in the Body of believers, but the spirit that is motivating us personally. If our spirit is wrong, we cannot properly receive the things of God. In fact, a wrong spirit always perverts the truths of God, causing confusion. Jesus told James and John that they did not know what spirit they were of when they wanted to call fire down from heaven on the Samaritans *(Luke 9:55).*

The final criterion that the Holy Spirit must meet is that of worship. There is no place in Scripture where it shows that man worships the Spirit of God. However, if the Spirit is God, then He would receive worship when the Father and Son are being rightly exalted and worshipped *(John 4:23-24)*. The other important key to the Spirit besides His character is that He is the one who sets up the proper environment for worship.

Only God would know how to worship in a proper way. A study on the Holy Spirit shows us that He is the One who enables us to pray and worship. For example, the disciples asked the Lord to teach them to pray. The woman at the well wanted to know about worship *(Luke 11:1; John 4:19-20)*. We are told to worship God in the right spirit and to pray in the Spirit *(John 4:23-24; 1 Corinthians 14:15; Ephesians 6:18)*. Clearly, the Spirit of God must set up the proper environment to ensure prayers that are effectual and worship that is acceptable.

Another aspect of the Spirit is that communion is associated to Him *(2 Corinthians 13:14)*. In other words, we cannot come into agreement or communion with the Father, except through the Holy Spirit *(Ephesians 2:16-18)*. He is the One that brings unity in the spirit at the point or place of Jesus and His redemption. Unity in the spirit is the environment where communion takes place not only between the Father and believers, but between the church members as well *(Ephesians 4:1-3)*.

Regardless of the confusion and debate over the Spirit, we can test a matter to see if He is the breath of inspiration behind it. Clearly, the environment becomes an expression of the spirit in operation. However, one of the greatest joys is that we can personally know the Holy Spirit. We do not have to be vague in our understanding regarding Him. He clearly expresses Himself in a way that He can be properly discerned. He is the One who signifies the new birth (seals us), regenerates (brings forth new life), transforms and renews the inner man (recreates), sanctifies (sets us apart for God's use), anoints (for service), and empowers believers (to be bold witnesses) *(Luke 4:18-19; John 3:3,5; Acts 1:8; Romans 12:1-2; 2 Corinthians 4:16; Ephesians 4:23; Titus 3:5; 1 John 2:27).*

The more Christians learn the character of the Holy Spirit through His work and manifestations, the sharper their discernment will become. As the Apostle Paul explained, the natural man can discern nothing in the spiritual realm. Only the Holy Spirit in each of us as believers is capable of discerning such matters *(1 Corinthians 2:10-14).*

The Spirit of God is what brings life to the Word of God *(John 6:63)*. If the Holy Spirit is not leading and guiding believers into the truths of God, the Word becomes dead letter *(Romans 7:6; 2 Corinthians 3:6)*. There will be no power for the Word to discern the spirit we are personally operating in, as well as cleanse us, transform, and ensure life. Only the Spirit of God can give each of us greater revelations of Jesus. Consider John in *Revelation.* He was in the Spirit when he received the incredible revelation about Jesus *(Revelation 1:10)*. Clearly, if we are of another spirit, we will never see, know, touch, or realize the Jesus of the Bible. We will end up believing in another Jesus.

Is it important to ensure that as believers we understand, operate within, and possess the correct spirit? It is easy to allow the confusions and abuses that surround the Holy Spirit to steer us away from coming to terms with His Person and work, but the Bible is clear that we must possess the right spirit to ensure the inward witness of our salvation.

The Word tells us that the Holy Spirit seals us until we can realize redemption in its fullness. In fact, He serves as the down payment in regards to our spiritual inheritance until redemption is fully realized *(Ephesians 13-14)*. It is the Spirit that bears witness that we are the children of God *(Romans 8:15-16)*. Obviously, as already pointed out it is the Spirit of God that bears record that we are saved *(1 John 3:24; 5:6-12)*. If the Holy Spirit is missing, there is no seal, no witness, and no record to verify our salvation. To believe that we are saved without this heavenly witness is to walk in denial of the truth or in delusion about the real testimony of God in regards to His Son and salvation. Therefore, the challenge is clear, we must know, interact with, and be able to discern the Spirit of God in the midst of the many counterfeits that are present in this world.

The Godhead

As we have studied and reasoned about the concept of the Father, the Son, and the Holy Spirit, there is nothing more we can do but conclude that all three Persons are God. In mathematical terms, this does not make sense. One plus one plus one does not equal one, yet the Word is clear that there is only one God. Now, either the Bible is true or it is the greatest joke in history. After all, many people are betting their eternal destination on this Book.

It has already been pointed out that as believers we must believe the whole Bible or discard all of it. We must consider it as truth in intent and purpose, or we must throw it out as nothing more than fables. Therefore, if we as believers are to believe the Word, there must be an explanation that will maintain the integrity of the complete Word of God without compromising the facts or revelations that are being advocated.

How can three persons equal one God? One of the terms that must be considered is the term "Godhead." The word "God" is clearly a reference to that which is deity, supreme, and mighty, but does the term "Godhead" encompass a greater revelation about the character of God?

According to "Strong's Exhaustive Concordance", "Godhead" means divinity. However, Godhead also points to deity or supreme Divinity. It is interesting to note that God has many references in the Old Testament to describe His character, but in the New Testament, the term Godhead is used in three Scriptures.

From the meaning of Godhead can we conclude that the Father, the Son, and the Holy Spirit are deity, but they function within or according to what can be referred to as supreme Divinity? This can all be quite confusing. To Scripturally reason this out, some type of premise or guidelines needs to be established in which to regard this subject;

The Bible gives us insight as to the premise or guidelines by telling us that God is identified by His nature *(Galatians 4:8)*. "Nature" is the essence of something, or in other words, it identifies who or what something is. Everything in creation has a nature that actually identifies it.

The makeup of something can be related to chemistry, rather than mathematics. Divinity points to the fact that God is divine by nature. This means He is supreme in all things. Could we say that within the essence or oneness of the Godhead are three Persons? These three persons are all deity or divine by nature; therefore, they are equal in status, character, power, and position.

"Equal" is a mathematical term. It means it is the same as, as far as nature, properties, quantity, and quality; therefore, three will always be equal to that which possesses the same properties, quantity, and quality. It is a matter of 1X1X1 equals itself and no matter how many times you times the number "one" with itself, it will always turn out to be "one."

Each person of the Godhead are equal to each other. They have the same nature, move into agreement with each other, and are one in plan and purpose. Jesus referred to this union and describe it as being one with the Father. For example, does this equality mean that the one true God manifests (makes apparent) Himself in three different personalities or persons?

For example, in *1 Timothy 3:16* we are told that God manifested Himself in the flesh. Does this mean that the character or nature of God operates in and through three persons or does it mean God simply reveals His person through three distinct personalities that somehow fades into one person or being? There is also the belief of Modalism, which has God manifesting Himself at different times in three distinct modes. However, Scripture refutes the last two concepts of the Godhead.

Jesus prayed to the Father. Obviously, He would pray to a distinct person other than Himself. He also would not be seeking the Father's will if there was no distinction or sovereignty between His will and the Father's will. At Jesus' baptism, all three persons of the Godhead were present but manifested themselves in different ways. Paul also distinguishes the Father and Son as being two distinct persons in *1 Corinthians 8:6.*

Based on these examples, it is safe to say that since personality points to the person of someone, that God manifests Himself in and through three persons. Obviously, these three Persons are equal in every way; and since deity or divine attributes are found in all three Persons of the Godhead, can we conclude that one true God is identified and made apparent in three Persons? For example, water always equals water regardless of its location, the size of the lake, ocean, or river, but it can manifest itself in three distinct ways, ice, fog and liquid. Clearly, water will always equal water, for it is what it is and it will never cease to be the complete sum of itself.

Obviously, these three Persons of the Godhead act independently from each other, but always in complete agreement with each other. This agreement would also mean that all three would work in compliance to one goal and purpose. Such agreement would be along the same lines as the concept of married couples becoming one flesh within the union of marriage *(Matthew 19:5-6; Ephesians 5:28-31).* Although the married husband and wife maintain their separate personalities, they are identified as being one in agreement, purpose, and heart. The fact that the Word of God identifies the Father, the Son, and the Holy Spirit as being divine by nature, and in total agreement in all matters could and would continually equal the sum total of what we refer to as the Godhead.

According to *Romans 1:20,* the concept of the Godhead is seen in the unseen aspects of creation. As you consider the idea of three in one, a good example is man. Within the human makeup of man are spirit, soul, and body, but we can't see his spirit or soul which defines him more than his body (*1 Thessalonians 5:23*). Each area has its different functions, but they work together as one unit.

You have the example of an egg which is made up of the yoke, egg white, and shell. Consider the petals of the Shamrock. These are just a couple of examples of how creation declares this truth, but the reality is that we have examples of this concept all around us.

As a result, we have this warning in *Romans 1:20, "For the invisible things of him from the creation of the world are clearly seen, being understood by the things that are made, even his eternal power and Godhead, so that they are without excuse."* (Emphasis added.) The harsh reality is that there will be no excuse as to why people did not believe and know the true God of heaven.

If there are three Persons that make up the Godhead, then we can understand some of the confusing Scriptures. For example, we have a reference to the plurality of the Godhead in such Scriptures as *Genesis 1:26; 3:22; 11:7;* and *Isaiah 6:8.* In each Scripture God makes reference to Himself with the words "our" and "us." We could say He is speaking to angels, but in a couple of these Scriptures it is clear He is speaking to those who are of His likeness or possess the same similitude, not to His created beings such as messengers (angels).

Clearly, we see how the Old and New Testaments approach the character and work of God from different angles, while producing the same picture. For example, the Old Testament shows God in His ways, but the New Testament explains the intent of His ways according to His character.

In the Old Testament, we have four Scriptures that clearly refer to the plurality of God, and in the New Testament, we have three Scriptures that reveal the concept of the Godhead to give us insight into this plurality. It is also important to point out that two or three witnesses confirm a matter *(Numbers 35:30; Deuteronomy 17:6; 19:15; Matthew 18:16).* A good example of this is that at Jesus' baptism John the Baptist, the Holy Spirit, and the Father, confirmed Jesus' identity as the Son of God and the Messiah. Consider *1 John 5:6-9.*

The New Testament also refers to this plurality of the Godhead by using the word "and." This word implies equality with, and is used in conjunction to something for the purpose of connecting the subject, thoughts, or terms. We see this word "and" connect the Father and Jesus together throughout the New Testament in character, purpose, and work.

Consider what the Bible tells us about the Godhead in *Acts 17:29-30, "Forasmuch then, as we are the offspring of God, we ought not to think that the Godhead is like unto gold, or silver, or stone, graven by art and man's device. And the times of this ignorance God winked at; but now commandeth all men everywhere to repent."*

What does man need to repent of according to *Acts*? He needs to repent of worshipping false gods. False gods find their idolatrous place in the heart and mind of man because he erects them in a place of importance and worship. The reason for such idolatry is that man is ignorant about the true God of heaven. Ignorance produces superstition about God. How many of our religious practices are nothing more than superstition? Therefore, man often worships God according to the darkness of his ignorance.

The point is, as Christians, we can know God, but we fail to seek Him. The natural response for most people is to look around for some religion or philosophy that feeds their religious pride, soothes their religious conscience, justifies their favorite religious concept, and confirms a certain religious emphasis. Obviously, such a search is not a matter of truth, but a matter of maintaining one's personal ignorance towards God. Because of man's insistence to maintain his own god, he clearly needs to repent about his attitude towards the true God of heaven.

How can we truly know God? *Colossians 2:9* answers this question, *"For in him dwelleth all the fullness of the Godhead bodily."* This Scripture is in reference to Jesus Christ. In Christ dwells all of the fullness of supreme divinity in bodily form. Was Jesus being a mere reflection of deity or does He possess the full nature of God and that His person is the express glory of the Godhead as *Hebrews 1:3* points out? A person cannot consistently reflect an image or thought. Ultimately, they will only reflect the inward character of their disposition. Therefore, Jesus could not reflect the essence of God unless He possessed God's very character and glory.

One of the confusing Scriptures in the Word of God is the one that says no man has seen God at any time, yet people in the Old Testament had actual encounters with God. For example, who was Abraham communicating with in regard to Sodom in *Genesis 18*?

There were three men who came to Abraham, two were identified as angels and the other one he addressed as Lord. Who did Jacob see at the top of the ladder between heaven and earth? He was referred to as LORD *(Genesis 28:12-13)*. Who did Moses, Aaron, Nadab, Abihu, and the seventy elders of Israel see in *Exodus 24:9-12*? They declared that they saw the God of Israel. Once again, we are reminded of what Isaiah witnessed in heaven in *Isaiah 6.* He declared that He saw the Lord.

Once again, consider *John 5:37.* Jesus stated that the people of Israel had not heard the voice of the Father nor seen His shape. The only way these incidents in the Old Testament would make sense is that Jesus is God. Since Jesus pre-existed as the Word (visible expression of God), He could have taken on the form of man or spoke to man in the Old Testament. If this is so, then these people of the Old Testament could rightly call Him Lord and declare that they had seen God.

If God is expressed through three persons, then it would mean that man would have to see all three persons of the Godhead to be able to declare that he had seen God. Since Jesus existed as the Word, was ordained to be the Son in the bosom of the Father, and fashioned as man, then we could reason that as Man, He is the only one in His humanity who has seen God in His unhindered glory.

The reason for mentioning the unhindered glory of God is due to Moses' experience in *Exodus 33:18-23.* Moses had communed with God for forty days and nights, but in *Exodus 33:18,* he makes this declaration, *"I beseech thee, show me thy glory."* The Lord responded by saying that no man could see His face (countenance-character-glory), and live *(Exodus 33:20).* Moses' request was honored, but he had to be put in the cleft of the rock, and then he could only see the back parts of the Lord.

Obviously, God is beyond our comprehension in our present state. Is there any way we can explain the depth of this incredible mystery as to the fact that God did become flesh? Is there any way we will be able to really understand God? The answer is clear, yet we can know this God who is beyond all comprehension by faith.

We cannot see Him in the fullness of His glory, but His glory has been revealed in His Son. We cannot see the fullness of His presence, but we can experience His presence in our lives through the Holy Spirit. However, it is up to each of us to seek God with all of our hearts *(Jeremiah 29:13; Amos 5:4-8).* The reason we must seek Him is that He is obscure. We see through a glass darkly *(1 Corinthians 13:12)*. In other words, we see through our flesh, which hinders our ability to see our great God. It is up to each of us to push through that which hinders us in our flesh, as well as the daunting influences of the world and man-made religion, so we can see the Jesus of the Bible, and know who He is for ourselves. Once we see Jesus for who He is and must be, we will be assured of seeing the fullness of the Godhead in bodily form.

Consider the following tables that reveals the work of each person of the Godhead in relationship to each other. However, for the Godhead to make sense, you must be willing to receive what the Word says by faith, which allows the Holy Spirit to reveal it to you as a truth that is so, regardless of whether it makes sense to our small-minded thinking.

Person	Point of Identification (2 Cor. 13:14)	Creation	Expression	Means of Salvation
The Father	Love (1 Jn. 3:1)	Designer (1 Cor 8:6)	Prophets/Son (He. 1:1-2)	Draws Jn. 6:44
The Son	Grace (Jn. 1:16)	Builder/Creator (Col. 1:15-18; Heb. 11:3)	The Word (Jn. 1:1; He. 11:3; Ps. 148:5)	Invites (Jn. 7:37-39)
Holy Spirit	Communion (Jn. 4:23-24)	Finish/Recreates (Ge. 1:2; Jb. 26:13)	The Ink (2 Co. 3:3)	Convicts (Jn. 16:7-11)
Believer	New Life (Ga. 2:20)	New Creation (2 Co. 5:17)	The Letter (2 Co. 3:2)	Believes (Ro. 10:9-10)

The Father is the One who designs, ordains, and establishes the way a matter must be. He sets forth the plan and pre-ordains how it will be brought forth for His glory. Everything the Son and the Holy Spirit do is in line with the Father's design, plan, and purpose.

Person	Goal of Salvation	Plan	Manifestation	Purpose
The Father	Reconciliation (Eph. 1:10; 2:16)	Do His Will (Mt. 12:46-50)	Relationship (Jn. 1:12)	Fellowship (1 Jn 1:3)
The Son	Redemption (Eph. 1:7)	Have His Mind (Phil. 2:5)	The Place (1 Co. 1:30)	Citizenship (Ep. 2:19)
The Holy Spirit	Born Again (Jn. 3:3, 5)	Empower (Acts 1:7-8)	Sanctification (1 Pe. 1:2)	Inheritance (Ep. 1:13-14)
Believer	Adoption (Ep. 1:5)	Method (Mt. 28:18-20)	Consecration (Ro. 12:1)	Identification (Ro. 6:4-5)

God's plan has always been about restoring the relationship that was lost in the Garden of Eden. To restore what was lost, there would have to be a point of reconciliation. The place of reconciliation can only occur upon redemption. It is for this reason the Father exalts the Son, the Son was lifted up, and the Holy Spirit leads people to Jesus because He is the only one who can bring forth reconciliation. We can get caught up with many great truths, but the red thread that runs through Scripture from the old to the new is redemption.[25]

---

[25] 2 Corinthians 5:18-21; Philippians 2:9-11; John 12:32; 16:13

Person	Communica-tion	Prayer	Desire	Church
The Father	Worship (Jo. 4:23)	As Father (Mt. 6:9)	Communion (Ex. 25:22)	Administrator (1 Co. 12:6)
The Son	Shepherd (Jn. 10:14)	Covenant (Jn. 14:6, 13)	Friendship Jn. 15:14-15	All in All Col. 3:11
The Holy Spirit	Revelation (Ep. 3:3)	Inspiration (Ep. 6:18)	Unity (Ep. 4:3)	Edifier (Ep. 4:12)
Believer	Disciple (Mt. 16:24)	Instrument (Ro. 6:13)	Know Him (Phil. 3:10)	Lively Stones (1 Pe. 2:5)

In Conclusion

As you can see, this challenge to discover God can prove to be difficult for those who are limited by their immaturity, but imagine how hard it might be for a former cult member to embrace the true God of heaven. Even in this study, we have waded through much, yet we have only skimmed the surface. There will always be some matters that remain fuzzy. In people's search to know God, they sometimes create more questions, but in the end, as believers we can trust our God that He will answer the questions of our heart in due time; that is, if we desire to know and love the truth.

People who have been members of a cult find it hard to trust God to unveil His truths because the Word was improperly handled and presented to them. Therefore, they have a tendency to reject truth in the areas where it has been abused or wrongly emphasized.

It is clear that those who have come out of a cult have been conditioned to rebel or reject any perception outside of what has been established. Since the foundation of what these poor souls believed has been torn up, there is nothing by which they can test a matter. Clearly, the kingdom of God has been closed to these people by heretical teachings and presentations. However, it does not have to remain closed. The truth of God and His Word can make them free—that is if they choose to love the truth and become vulnerable before it.

The question will remain the same for each of us concerning spiritual matters. Do we really want the truth? The truth can prove to be bitter to the stomach when it comes to actually digesting it, salty (burning) to wounds, harsh to our vulnerable spots, and sharp to the weak areas of our theology *(Jeremiah 23:29; Acts 4:10-12; Revelation 10:9-10)*. The problem is that after the improper handling of the Word that has been used to wound people in cults, there are now trigger points that can be activated by different subjects found in the Word of God.

These trigger points cause these individuals to shy away, rebel, disregard, or slam the particular truth that is being presented. Needless to say, the Word is stripped of its power to bring proper instruction, healing, and liberty to these wounded people.

Such people often become selective about the Word, producing ears that desire to be tickled, rather than challenged *(2 Timothy 4:2-3)*. Ultimately, they will seek counterfeits that will make them feel good about their life, their anger, and their personal justifications for their cynical attitudes towards the matters of God.

The Word of God is clear about all spiritual matters, but we each must approach it to believe it is true, regardless of how unpleasant or challenging it may be. After all, the Word will stand when the fires of judgment consume all else. Therefore, we need to choose to simply believe it is true, and know everything will be properly explained in light of the fullness of Jesus' redemption. Meanwhile as Christians, we have the assurance that in time the true teacher of the Bible will illuminate it to our spirits to bring forth the necessary transformation to our minds.

The problem that remains is unbelief, which can plague each of us at different times. However, it can prove to be even harder for former cult members to trust anything after finding out that people who supposedly were guarding their souls duped them.

Such disillusioned individuals have a tendency to give way to feelings about how a matter affects them, personal conclusions when it comes to the Word, and skepticism and scrutiny towards religious matters that do not make sense to them. Rather than being properly discerned, sound teaching comes under the scrutiny of these people's critical eye, causing its purity to be challenged by suspicion, and its simplicity to be mocked.

As we as believers contend for the true faith in the midst of grave unbelief, we have to come to a conclusion that the conflict does not rest with the Word of God, but with man's presentation. One thing that we humans are good at is putting certain emphasis or terminology on something to explain it. What causes conflict is the wrong emphasis or terminology.

For example, much about God is discredited because of the popular term "doctrine of the Trinity" that is used to explain the concept of the Godhead. There are a couple of reasons for the conflict. The first one is that the concept of the Godhead is not a doctrine, but a truth. Doctrine can be changed, disregarded, or ignored, but a truth is something that we must receive by faith, and apply to the attitude we are developing about God and how we are to approach Him.

The second problem with this term is that it appears to originate within Catholicism. However, it was not the Roman Catholics who coined this term but Tertullian.

He was born in 150 A.D. before the conception of the initial (old) Catholic Church under Cyprian in the third century and the establishment of what we now know to be the Roman Catholic Church in the fourth century.[2] Tertullian was fluent in Greek and Latin. He was the first to coin the term "trinity" to explain the

---

[2] The Pilgrim Church; E. H. Broadbent, © 1999; Gospel Folio Press, pgs. 34, 43-47

86

concept of the Godhead to the western Christians who only knew Latin.[3]

Clearly, the concept of the "trinity" was a belief of the first Christians. The first vicar or pope of the Roman Catholic Church, Constantine, no doubt adopted the concept of the Godhead when he combined Christian beliefs with pagan practices. Moreover, just because the Roman Church has taken an established Christian belief and instituted it into their belief system does not make that belief wrong. In fact, if you study the lives of many of the great reformers, including those who made sure the common people had God's Word made available to them, some were committed believers that recognized the difference between the traditions of the Catholic Church and the truths and teachings of the Word of God. Many of the reformers paid with their very lives for choosing to believe God's Word over a religious system.

As Christians, we do not test something according to how other people have handled a belief or truth, but according to its original source. The concept of the Godhead is found in Scripture. Regardless of how others may have tried to describe or explain it, it does not discredit its validity. It is up to each of us as believers to test out all matters in light of Scripture and to choose to believe it on the basis that it is found in the Word of God.

Obviously, it is easy for people to pick and choose what they will believe. However, as someone once said, "ff God said it, it is not for us to debate it; rather it is up to each of us to choose to believe it as being true." It is our sole responsibility as Christians to test whether something is of God. Regardless of the instrument used or how it is presented, it is our responsibility to see if a matter is being inspired by the throne of heaven. If it is

---

[3] A Glimpse at Early Christian Church Life; Tertullian, ©1991 by David W. Bercot, pg. 2

of God, we must receive it by faith. Active faith will act upon a matter, allowing the Spirit of God to bring confirmation of the truth and revelation of it to our spirit.

As Christians, will we accept the challenge to possess the faith first delivered to the saints, or will we allow Satan to rob us of truth, kill our testimony of the true God, and destroy the faith that ends in salvation (*Jude 3*)? It will be a personal choice on our part as to what master we serve. The master we serve will inspire the type of attitudes we develop towards God's ways, His truth, and the life that He is offering to each of us (*John 14:6*).

After considering this section, has your perception of God changed? If so, explain in what way.

Section 3

THE ISSUE OF SALVATION

WHAT DOES IT MEAN
TO BE SAVED?

One cannot help but think that if a person's perception is wrong about God, then they must have an incorrect perception about salvation. What does it mean to be saved? Clearly, this matter lies at the heart of fundamental Christianity, and must be properly addressed to counteract the cult mentality. Rather than assume or presume we understand the matter of salvation, we must answer this question, especially since our eternal destination rests on this issue.

To most people the issue of salvation comes down to saying a prayer. This prayer simply invites someone by the name of Jesus to save the individual from condemnation. However, does a prayer save a person, or does the Person of Jesus Christ save the individual?

Obviously, we need to clarify what it means to be saved. When you look up salvation or being saved, it means to be delivered from something. Clearly, if people are being delivered from something, one can only reason that we each need to understand what we are being saved or delivered from.

Another important aspect is that the Word of God talks about this deliverance in regards to the past, present, and future. What do we need to be delivered from that affects our past, present, and future? To gain a glimpse into our deliverance, we must consider the Gospel.

Romans 1:16 makes this statement about salvation, *"For I am not ashamed of the gospel of Christ; for it is the power of God unto salvation to everyone that believeth; to the Jew first, and also to the Greek."* The Gospel, or good news, is the power of God unto salvation.

Therefore, to understand salvation, we must come to terms with the Gospel. When we speak of the Gospel, most people think of *John 3:16, "For God so loved the world, that he gave his only begotten Son, that whosoever believeth in him should not perish, but have everlasting life."* This Scripture stipulates that mankind is in trouble and out of benevolence, God gave His only begotten Son to save us from the inevitable. However, what is God saving each of us from? Clearly, *John 3:16* lays a foundation, or serves as a prelude to the Gospel.

A summary of the Gospel can be found in *1 Corinthians 15:1-4.* The essence of the Gospel is that Jesus died for our sins, He was buried and three days later, He rose from the grave. Why is this message so powerful? There are three major points to the Gospel. 1) It identifies the problem that is plaguing man. 2) This message tells us in what way the problem was dealt with. 3) And, it shows us that Jesus was successful in His mission.

Obviously, we must come to terms with this powerful message that God is using to save the souls of people. But, for the purpose of examining our own understanding about this message, we must consider what the Gospel means to us individually. Write down what this message means to you.

Sin

The problem that plagues man can be identified in the small three-letter word "sin." Sin is defined as "offense." In other words, our great Judge God has been offended because we have trespassed His Law in some way or broken the covenant. Before we deal with this subject, it is important for each person to consider how they see sin. In fact, because of sin all men are facing the wrath of God, which will be directed towards all that walk in iniquity *(Matthew 1:21; Romans 1:18; 5:9, 21; 6:20; Ephesians 2:1-3; 1 Thessalonians 1:10).* What is sin to you?

There are two major affronts against the Gospel. The first affront is against Jesus. Jesus is able to save us to the utmost because of who He is *(Hebrews 7:25).* If a person possesses a different Jesus from what the Word of God advocates, such a Jesus will not be able to save the person.

The second affront against the Gospel is the fact that people have been trying to do away with sin. Sin has been watered down or completely done away with by clothing it in terms that take away its harsh reality. For example, sins are considered mistakes, diseases, and alternative lifestyles that are natural or inherited.

In some ways, these conclusions are right, but they are not being used in the correct perspective. For example, it is a mistake to make light of sin in any way. Sin is not a mistake; rather it is a natural preference of man in his present, fallen state. It is a disease in the sense that it destroys man's relationship with God, thereby, destroying his soul as well. However, man can be healed from its destructive ways.

Sin also points to a lifestyle, but it is one of choice or preference. Due to sin, the state of death has been passed down to all men. Death, not life is man's future inheritance in light of eternity, but it is one inheritance that can be changed *(Romans 5:12).*

How does sin affect us? Sin affects us in three ways: disposition, walk, and works. Sin abounds in its consequences, influences, and activities. Ultimately, sin causes us to reject and rebel against God's authority, walk in delusion about God, and in denial about its effects in our lives. Let us now consider these effects of sin on our lives. This is vital if we are to understand what we are being delivered from.

Disposition

Man is in a fallen condition because of Adam's rebellion against God *(Romans 5:12)*. This fallen condition is not based on who man is, but what he fails to become. In other words, man is human by nature. This will not change, but what man allows himself to become as far as the character or inner state of his being comes down to who or what he allows himself to be influenced by. What is your understanding about the inner state of man?

"Disposition" represents the inner state of man. This inner state is reflected through each of our attitudes towards God and life. Ultimately, it will be manifested in our lives by the type of fruit that is being produced *(Matthew 7:16-20)*. *Romans 3:23* tells us how our disposition was affected by sin, *"For all have sinned, and come short glory of God."* The first man was created to reflect the glory of God in the midst of creation.

Man's initial disposition or state was that of innocence before God. He had communion with God, thereby, he had the ability to reflect the influence of God to the rest of creation. This was brought out in the case of Moses. After being in the presence of God, his countenance shone with the manifestation of God's presence and glory *(Exodus 34:29-35; 2 Corinthians 3:7)*.

When Adam gave in to rebellion, his inner state became marred. He became soulish or selfish in his disposition. It was no longer about establishing his life in God, but now it was about finding his own life outside of God. His state no longer reflected the influence of God, but now it would reflect the darkness of a soul that was separated from the one who is the essence of true, lasting light. After all, it is the light of God that served as man's life *(John 1:4)*. However, now man was in darkness. He would taste the consequences of his sin: that of death.

Man would experience death in two ways. Spiritually, he became separated from God, who is the essence of all life. Since man was spiritually dead, he no longer was inclined towards God. The Apostle Paul put it best in *Romans 3:11, "There is none that understandeth, there is none that seeketh after God."*

Due to sin man was now lost to God and in a quagmire of uselessness as he pursued that which was attractive and desirous to his way of thinking and doing. However, such pursuits would prove to be vanity and bitterness to the soul since all such pursuits were all under a curse of death and destruction *(Genesis 3:17-19; Romans 6:23; 8:18-25; Galatians 3:10-13).* Not only did man taste spiritual death as he walked according to darkness, he would taste physical death as well.

Since man's inner state had changed from experiencing the life of God to walking in the state of death, he was no longer inclined towards the one true God. In fact, he possessed no real desire towards the God of heaven. His desires were directed elsewhere.

He now ceased to value the spiritual aspect of a life that found its satisfaction and purpose in communing with his Creator. However, man was created with a need to worship God. Since Adam's defiant act separated all men from their true Creator, their natural tendency would be to erect a god of their own liking that would justify their selfish ambitions and pursuits. The main god that is erected is self—the image, the intellect, the rights, the arrogance, and self-sufficiency of self. In short, man's religion and focus of worship would become man-centered, rather than God-centered. We call the exaltation of man in this way, "humanism."

Needless to say, idolatry has caused man to become ignorant towards God. Man has religion, but it often reveals superstition about God and not knowledge of the true God. Man has his theology, but it often lacks life, authority, and power. Man worships, but he does not know whom he is really worshipping. Man has many altars, but few are dedicated to the real God, nor do they show sacrifices that are acceptable and worthy of who

He is *(Matthew 15:3-9; John 4:22-24; Acts 17:22-34; Hebrews 13:15-16)*.

The other aspect of sin is its deception *(Hebrews 3:13)*. Since man is often the subject of his own worship, he cannot possibly see the vanity and destruction of his man-centered religion. Since man's search ends with his own conclusions, he cannot see how he can be wrong about present matters. Since man often compares himself with others who are considered more miserable in their plight, he becomes the final authority in all matters. *Proverbs 14:12* and *16:25* states there is a way that seems right to man, but it leads to death and destruction.

It is hard for man, in his state of self-exaltation, to realize that his ways of doing are perverted towards God. His conclusions often come out of vain imaginations that exalt themselves against the real knowledge of God; and his attempts to take care of a matter amount to nothing more than vanity *(Proverbs 21:8; 2 Corinthians 10:4-5; Ecclesiastes 13:8, 13-14)*.

The Word of God commands us to let the mind or attitude of Jesus be in us. Jesus' disposition was that of lowliness. It was expressed in an attitude of meekness *(Matthew 11:28; Philippians 2:5)*. Once again, we are reminded that we must take on a new disposition that will change our attitude and approach towards God. In fact, the first four Scriptures in *Philippians 2* reveals how such a disposition will express itself in our lives, while *Philippians 2:6-8* shows how it expressed itself in Jesus' life.

Our nature as man is who we are, but our disposition will determine who we become. In other words, who or what we will express in our lives daily.

This brings us to how man lives or walks out his life.

The Flesh

The first man was created as a spiritual being with the very breath of God in him *(Genesis 2:7)*. In other words, he was given the breath or Spirit of God to interact with his Creator, who is Spirit and truth *(John 4:23-24)*. When Adam rebelled in the Garden of Eden, the breath of God lifted from him, closing down the spiritual aspect of his life. Instead of being able to operate on a spiritual plane, he became soulish or fleshly in his way of doing, thinking, and being. Instead of the matters of the soul (the will, mind, and emotions) being influenced and directed by the Spirit towards the matters of God, they became subject to the pursuits, desires, and affections of fleshly appetites as he began to interact with the physical world around him. In man's attempt to get the world around him to feed and satisfy his inner being, he has become enslaved to it (*2 Timothy 2:4; James 4:4; 1 John 2:15-17*).

Man, in an unregenerate state, walks according to the flesh. According to the Apostle Paul in *Romans 7:18*, there is no good thing in the flesh. To put this into perspective, we must understand what goodness is. Only God is good *(Matthew 19:17)*.

This means that all that originates with God is beneficial. It has the ability to bring pleasure, well-being, beauty, and substance to the person's life. In light of this information, the Apostle Paul stated that anything inspired or originating in the flesh cannot be considered good, because it will not benefit or add to the person's well-being. He confirmed this truth in *Romans 3:12, "They are all gone out of the way, they are together become unprofitable; there is none that doeth good, no, not one."* What does it mean for you and me to walk according to the flesh? (Be sure to write your answer or conclusion to the question to see how well you do understand these issues.)

Galatians 5:21 tells us those who walk according to the works of the flesh will not inherit the kingdom of God. The flesh is not spiritual; therefore, it cannot receive the things of God, without perverting or tainting them *(Romans 8:5-8; 1 Corinthians 2:13-14)*. However, the flesh tries to become spiritual on an intellectual (thinking great things) or an emotional level (the wave of emotional sentiment and experience). Such attempts open people up to the realm of Satan, rather than God.

It is not unusual to see people try to rehabilitate the flesh. They try to reform according to standards; they comply to what they perceive is right. They strive to perform according to requirements; and, they adjust to give the appearance that all is well. However, it is all outward attempts. The inward environment remains unchanged.

As you honestly consider the motivation, the influence, and the activities of the flesh, you realize why the Apostle Paul quoted the Old Testament Scripture: *"As it is written, There is none righteous, no, not one" (Romans 3:10).* Righteousness points to that which is holy and just. It implies that a person's character and actions are coming from a point of innocence or purity. Since the flesh is selfish and self-serving, there is no innocence or purity in it. Therefore, it fails to be upright before God in motivation and action. All that comes from the flesh has already been judged, and will stand condemned. This is also in reference to what we consider good works.

Works

We now come to the issue of good works, and the emphasis that can be improperly put on them. As previously stated, almost all cults have one thing in common. They put a tremendous emphasis on good works. What kind of emphasis do you think works play in the Christian walk?

Most people judge themselves by their works. They believe that if they are doing good works, there must be something good in them. This shows their ignorance towards God. He does not consider us according to our works, but according to our inward disposition.

If our inward disposition is that of selfishness, then the purpose for personal good works would be self-centered. For instance, people do things because they want to feel good about themselves, do away with guilt, or earn recognition. Clearly, this is man-centered, not God-centered. It will bring glory to man, not God. Since it is not God-centered, it is not eternal, satisfying, or rewarding.

The Word of God clearly outlines this reality. In *Isaiah 64:6,* it tells us our best is as filthy rags. *Titus 1:15-16* tells us how to the pure all things are pure, but to the defiled and unbelieving their mind and conscience are defiled. Even though profane people may profess they know God, their works show their true spiritual condition. It refers to their works as being reprobate or useless.

Matthew 7:21-23 brings this subject closer to home. Apparently, there will be those on judgment day who will bring up their works before the Lord. However, as believers, we are not justified by works, but by faith *(Romans 4:2-3).* In fact, what is not the product of faith is sin *(Romans 14:23b).* It is our faith towards God that is pleasing to Him, not our works *(Hebrews 11:6).* Although these individuals in *Matthew 7:21-23* will make reference to works, Jesus will not recognize them. He commands them to depart from Him because they worked iniquity, rather than doing the will of the Father.

The final reality about works is found in *1 Corinthians 3:12-15.* Paul tells us all works will be tested by fire. This fire will determine the quality of the works. The quality of works brings us back to whether they are ordained, sanctioned, and blessed by God.

Some works will come forth as gold (pure), silver (redemptive) or precious stones (costly). While other works will be exposed as wood (self-righteous works), hay (worldly inspired), and stubble (inspired by the flesh). Needless to say, the wood, hay, and stubble will be consumed in the fires of judgment, but the person will be saved by fire.

Ultimately, all acceptable works will be from God, bring glory to Him, and will be offered back to Him on judgment day. If the flesh, world, or man's religion is associated with any work, it will be considered useless and designated for judgment.

As we consider the indictment against the flesh, we realize why Jesus had to die for us. We are most hopeless and miserable in our plight. We can delude ourselves based on fleshly works, we can justify our selfishness because we think that we deserve happiness, and we can convince ourselves we are not so bad because we are religious. However, the truth is we remain miserably lost unless we receive Jesus as our only hope and solution.

Redemption

The next part of the Gospel is that Jesus died for us. Jesus' death on the cross points to redemption. *Psalm 49:8* tells us the redemption of our souls is precious. Redemption is a theme that runs through the Bible. What does redemption mean to you?

As we study the harsh reality of our plight, we realize that without intervention, we are doomed in our sins. Obviously, man cannot deliver himself from his plight. He lives in an environment of death, where sin abounds; therefore, the activities of sin can consume him. He is a slave to the works, consequences, dictates, and appetites of sin, which are constantly taking him captive *(Romans 5:20-21; 6:20-23; James 1:13-15)*.

How can people be delivered from this terrible doom? The only one who could save any of us from our spiritual plight is

God. To satisfy the Law of God, the judgment upon sin would have to be carried out. *Hebrews 9:22* tells us there is no remission of sin without the shedding of blood. Remission points to pardon. We must receive a pardon to be released from the consequences of sin.

In the Old Testament animal sacrifices were offered to make atonement for sin. This simply meant that sin was covered by the blood of these sacrifices, but sin was never taken away. Therefore, these sacrifices could not satisfy the judgment on sin. *Hebrews 10:4* confirms this, *"For it is not possible that the blood of bulls and of goats should take away sins."*

It was not enough to cover the sins; they had to be remitted in order to receive a pardon. Therefore, someone had to be willing to take our place as our substitute to satisfy the Law. This means the substitute must satisfy the judgment pronounced by the Law to its fullest degree. In the case of humanity, man stood cursed by the Law, and the sentence over him was that of spiritual death *(Romans 6:23; Galatians 3:13)*. In our case the substitute would have to die in our place to ensure our release from the curse and judgment that hung over each of our heads.

God's plan was to provide the one sacrifice that would satisfy judgment and bring reconciliation between Him and man. As God did in Israel, He would use the death of the first born of Egypt to bring about the necessary release from slavery. Only this time, He would offer up His only begotten Son. Ultimately, it would be God's way of redeeming or buying back His people from the taskmasters of the Law, sin, the world, and Satan *(Exodus 12:12-13; John 3:16-18; Galatians 3:13; 1 Corinthians 6:20; 7:23; Ephesians 2:13-17)*.

Hence, enters Jesus Christ on the scene. *1 John 2:1-2* tells us that Jesus is our advocate and the propitiation for our sins. Jesus became our advocate. This does not mean He is simply our defense attorney, but rather He serves as our very defense in the courts of heaven. Because He took our place and paid the complete sentence for our offences committed against God and His Law, He is able to plead our cause.

The fact that we have been bought back points to the fact that God is now our owner. We do not belong to the world, Satan, or ourselves. We are citizens of heaven, and as our owner, Jesus is our Lord *(Ephesians 2:19; Philippians 2:9-11; 3:20)*. The real issue here is whom we decide to serve. Jesus may be our Lord, but we must choose to come under His authority and obey Him. This requires complete consecration on our part. However, many of us have divided loyalties, maintain personal rights, and will determine in what way we will serve Jesus.

The reason for such division in our loyalties and servitude is that very few of us truly have become identified with Jesus. This brings us to the next part of the Gospel. Jesus died for our sins and was buried.

Identification

Why is identification of the utmost importance concerning our Christian life? We each need to meditate upon this question before we answer it.

You might wonder in what way Jesus' burial is associated with identification. Everything Jesus did was to identify with man. He was tempted in every way as we are, but without sin. He tasted the challenges of the flesh, but remained in submission to the Father. He was weary, yet He became a place of rest as He calmed the seas and the turmoil of man's heart. He experienced death, so man could possess life. Jesus became identified with man in his sinful plight, so man could become identified with God in His righteousness *(Matthew 11:28-30; 26:36-46; 2 Corinthians 5:21; Hebrews 4:16)*.

The Apostle Paul made reference to this identification in *Romans 6:3-14*. Jesus became sin, or the sin offering to take our sins to the grave with Him *(2 Corinthians 5:21)*. There, these sins would lose their power and influence over our lives. However, we must realize that the message of the cross represents the great exchange. It is not enough to take something away; it must be replaced by something else. The power and influence of sin must be exchanged for a new life. This new life will be the life of Christ. However, this exchange must be marked by death.

The grave clothes in Jesus' day marked the end to the previous life. In Lazarus' resurrection in *John 11,* Jesus commanded the people to loose him from the grave clothes, and let him go. The old life marks oppression, hopelessness, and death. Jesus came to release the hold that the old has on each of us, but there must be a death, a burial, and a loosening from the old.

In water baptism we see the symbolism of the grave. We are taken into the water (grave), and are washed clean (of sins). Therefore, the sins are left in the grave, and when we are brought up out of the water, we are being brought forth in a new life. However, the grave clothes of the old way of thinking, doing, and being can still cling to us. We must also be loosed from them.

The Word of God shows us we have a responsibility to do away with the old. Commands such as mortifying and putting off are associated with the old life *(Ephesians 4:22-24; Colossians 3:5-9). 1 Peter 2:1-2* tells us we must lay aside all malice (hatred), guile (deception), hypocrisies (feigning something), envies (jealousies), and evil speaking (gossip, slander, sarcasm, crude comments etc.), and begin to desire the pure milk (doctrine) of the Word. Obviously, if we try to partake of the pure milk of the Word without first getting rid of the old, it will be defiled.

Just as Jesus died to secure our redemption, we must die daily to the power and influence of sin in our lives. This death means that sin no longer can attract or bring us into bondage. Since the new life that is being established in us by faith is the actual life of the Son of God, sin will continue to lose its power, influence, and attraction in our lives. Ultimately, the mind or disposition of Jesus will be established in us. We will walk in meekness and humility before God, ready to come into submission to Him in all matters *(Luke 9:23-24; Galatians 2:20; Philippians 2:5).*

Such a life is also a life of consecration. Consecration means a person is separating themself from that which is unholy, so they can be separated unto God, and walk in a life that reflects the glory of Christ in disposition, attitude, and conduct.

Obviously, Jesus went to the grave so we could experience freedom from the old way of doing and being. Such freedom allows us to embrace the new and come under the leading, authority, and power of the Holy Spirit in our lives. It is under the leading and power of the Holy Spirit that deeds of the body will be completely mortified, and the inner man will be transformed *(Romans 8:13; 12:1-2).* The result is that we will actually put on the Lord Jesus Christ *(Romans 13:14).*

Identification will allow believers to realize the significance of the last part of the Gospel message—that of resurrection power.

Resurrection

The final part of the Gospel is that three days after being put in the grave, Jesus rose from it. It is important that as Christians we understand why resurrection is important. What do you think the significance of resurrection is in the Christian life?

The Apostle Paul summarized the importance of the resurrection in this way, *"And if Christ be not raised, your faith is vain; ye are yet in your sins" (1 Corinthians 15:17).*

As you study resurrection in Scripture, you will begin to realize how important this issue is. Jesus talked much about resurrection. He told the Sadducees, who did not believe in resurrection, that they erred because they did not know the Scriptures, or the power of God *(Matthew 22:29-30).*

Scripture shows us that every person will be resurrected. However, in *John 5:29*, Jesus speaks of two types of resurrection, *"And shall come forth; they that have done good, unto the resurrection of life; and they that have done evil, unto the resurrection of damnation."* As you study what is good, you realize it is associated with God, but evil is associated with the works of the flesh, the world, and Satan. Once again, it comes down to who a person is serving.

The prophet Daniel said this about resurrection in *Daniel 12:2, "And many of those who sleep in the dust of the earth shall awake, some to everlasting life, and some to shame and everlasting contempt."*

Man was created to live forever, but as to the state in which he will exist or live comes down to what he does with Jesus Christ. It is not God's heart to see man live in a state of eternal damnation. It is God's will that all be raised up to eternal life *(John 5:39-40)*. He provided resurrection power that resides within man through His Spirit.

This resurrection power (internal power) will respond to the voice of Jesus and raise up those who believe the Gospel unto everlasting life, while those who are devoid of this internal power will be raised up to eternal damnation. Such power will be an external power that comes from above and not from within. Clearly, it is man's choice as to where he will spend his eternal existence.

Jesus identified this resurrection power in *John 11:25-26, "Jesus said unto her, I am the resurrection, and the life; he that believeth in me, though he were dead, yet shall he live: And whosoever liveth and believeth in me shall never die. Believest thou this?"* The Spirit and reality of Jesus' life in us as believers serve as the source and hope of resurrection power that will raise each of us into eternal life.

Jesus' resurrection proved a couple of major points. First, we serve a risen Savior and Lord. No other religious leader has ever been raised from the dust of the earth, except Jesus. He now sits on the right hand of the Father as our High Priest *(Ephesians 1:19-20; Colossians 3:1; Hebrews 7:17; 8:1).*

The Apostle Paul in his summary of Jesus Christ in *1 Timothy 3:16* talks about Him being received up into glory. Of course, we have the promise that He will return in the same way He ascended *(Acts 1:10-11).* Clearly, His resurrection verifies His identity, works, message, and the blessed hope of Him coming back for His Body, the Church.

Another aspect of Jesus' resurrection is that He proved to be victorious over the works of the enemy. The Apostle Paul made this declaration in *1 Corinthians 15:55, "O death, where is thy sting? O grave, where is thy victory?"*

Since believers have resurrection power, they have the ability to overcome. The Apostle Paul stated that, *"For if we have been planted together in the likeness of his death, we shall be also in the likeness of his resurrection" (Romans 6:5).*

In *1 Corinthians 15:52-53,* the Apostle Paul declared that when we are raised in the newness of the complete life of Jesus, the corruptible (the flesh) will have been put off, and the incorruptible (the fullness of the life of Jesus) put on. Even King David realized that he would eventually be changed into the likeness of his Creator, *"As for me, I will behold thy face in righteousness; I shall be satisfied when I awake, with thy likeness" (Psalm 17:15).*

The Apostle Paul put resurrection in this light in *Philippians 3:10, "That I may know him, and the power of his resurrection, and the fellowship of his sufferings, being made conformable unto his death."* Paul's heart desire was to know Jesus and to experience the power of His resurrection. However, He was aware this knowledge could not occur unless he was willing to know the fellowship of His sufferings. In the end, he became identified with Jesus in His death.

Revelation 20:6 tells us, *"Blessed and holy is he that hath part in the first resurrection; on such the second death hath no power, but they shall be priests of God and of Christ, and shall reign with him a thousand years."* As we already know, there are two types of resurrection. The first resurrection will be unto eternal life, the second to eternal damnation. John is clearly distinguishing that we need to be sure to be part of the first resurrection, and not the latter.

The responsibility to examine ourselves in light of resurrection is a necessity. Do we possess the real Jesus? After all, it is only the Jesus of the Bible who possesses both the resurrection power and the life.

If Christ is in us, then we can be sure of the promise found in *Ephesians 2:5-6, "Even when we were dead in sins, hath quickened us together with Christ, (by grace ye are saved;) And hath raised us up together, and made us sit together in heavenly places in Christ Jesus."* Believers have already been raised up in position in high places in Jesus. It is a matter of time before they will experience the fullness of His resurrection power and life in them.

WHAT IS SALVATION?

Has your understanding of salvation changed after studying the previous information? If so, explain in what way it has changed.

Once again, we must remind ourselves that salvation to most people is nothing more than a sinner's prayer. Granted, one must ask Jesus to save them before He can step on the scene as their Savior. However, salvation entails more than just a prayer. *Romans 10:9-10* gives us this insight into salvation, *"That if thou shalt confess with thy mouth the Lord Jesus, and shalt believe in thine heart that God hath raised him from the dead, thou shalt be saved. For with the heart man believeth unto righteousness; and with the mouth confession is made unto salvation."*

Obviously, salvation is more than a sinner's prayer; it is a heart revelation of what Jesus did for us. He took our place on the cross, but the grave could not hold Him. He died so that we could be delivered from that which is oppressive and destructive. He rose from the dead. His complete work of redemption and the reconciliation with God that it leads to, points to the Gospel and its glorious power to deliver us *(Romans 1:16)*.

As we consider the concept of deliverance, we must recognize it is in regards to sin. We have been saved from the consequences of sin, that of death (past), we are being saved from the influence and workings of sin (the flesh) in our present life, and we will be saved from all of the activities and judgment of sin (eternal separation) that abound in this world in the future.

Such a heart revelation will not stop with the realization of what Christ did. It will make an exchange as to who will now be our master. Since sin has been taken away by Jesus' death, it no longer can serve as a master that brings us into the entanglements of the world and into the unmerciful claws of Satan. In our deliverance we now have the freedom to choose our master. In our new-found freedom, we acknowledged our new Lord by confessing, "The Lord Jesus Christ."

As stated, "Lord" means Jesus is my owner and I am His servant. As I grow in the knowledge of Jesus, I will become a bondservant. A bondservant is one who chooses to become a servant for life out of love for their master. You can read about this bondservant in *Deuteronomy 15.*

Like the servants in this reference, believers have been redeemed (set free) from being servants of harsh taskmasters. However, since we, as Christians, must serve something, we can see the benefit of serving our Lord Jesus Christ the rest of our lives. Such a consecrated service will be earmarked by the power, presence, anointing, and distinction of the Holy Spirit.

Now that we understand that salvation begins with the Lord Jesus Christ, we must come to terms with what it means to believe in the heart the salvation message.

Faith

Ephesians 2:8 tells us we are saved by grace through faith. What does this mean to you?

Grace is God's part in our salvation. This means He shows us undue favor by freely offering us the gift of life. Faith is our response. Faith is active and simply believes what the Word declares about a matter, and receives it in the heart as truth *(Romans 10:17)*. Clearly, God's grace can only be realized through faith. As we respond to God in sincere faith, we will properly receive His grace. In fact, all that God does for us is a matter of His grace. In addition, it is only as we receive God's favor by faith, that God's grace can flow freely through every area of our spiritual lives *(John 1:16-17; Romans 1:17)*.

Keep in mind the heart represents the understanding, will, and emotions. All three point to our disposition towards God. Receiving the truth of the Gospel does not mean that we will understand the total implications of Jesus' death, burial, and resurrection. However, what it does mean is we will have a sense of our need to receive the truth of the Gospel as our solution to the problem of our spiritual plight.

Faith is a choice of the will. Choosing to believe often requires us to bypass personal understanding and redirect our affections and emotions to come into agreement with a matter.

Once we believe the Gospel, faith of this nature is accounted as righteousness on our part, and we are born again from above *(John 3:3, 5; Romans 4:3, 9)*. This means we are given a new heart and a new spirit, pointing to a new disposition, making us into new creations *(Jeremiah 32:39-40; Ezekiel 36:26-27; 2 Corinthians 5:17; Hebrews 10:15-16)*.

The new heart is a heart inclined towards God. It is pliable under God; therefore, He is able to influence it by the Holy Spirit writing His laws upon the heart, making them revelation and life. Such revelations will establish in greater measure the life of Christ in the believer.

Active faith must not simply be considered a "work"; rather, it is a sincere and natural response to grace. In fact, a measure of faith is given by God *(Romans 12:3)*. It is an act of grace on His part. The Apostle Paul is clear that we are saved by grace through faith and not by any personal works. Deliverance is truly an act of grace on God's part. Faith will respond to God's grace through obedience to the truth that is being advocated. Such obedience will result in good works.

Scripture shows us we are not saved by works; rather we are saved unto good works. What constitutes good works?

Ephesians 2:10 gives us this insight, *"For we are his workmanship, created in Christ Jesus unto good works, which God hath before ordained that we should walk in them."* First, good works have been ordained by God. Therefore, these works are from God, of God, and for God, thereby, making a person perfect, complete, or mature in every good work *(Hebrews 13:21)*.

We are told that God is able to make all grace abound towards us to ensure that we have what is necessary in all things so we can abound in good works *(2 Corinthians 9:8)*. In other words, God blesses and equip us to ensure we flourish in the good works He has ordained. We are also instructed to walk worthy of the Lord, which will not only please Him, but such a walk will prove to be fruitful in every good work.

Clearly, not all works are fruitful or pleasing. In fact, doing what is acceptable and pleasing to God is our reasonable service, but there are times that doing good to others actually serves as a sweet sacrifice to our Lord *(Romans 12:1-2; Hebrews 13:15-16)*.

James declared that he would show his faith by his works. In other words, works are a natural response of sincere faith and will accompany salvation *(Hebrews 6:9)*. As Christians we do not do these works to gain merits or recognition; rather we do these works because we believe and love God, and we know they are not only a matter of our reasonable service, but they are the right thing to do.

Self-Denial

Jesus talked about what it would mean to be His disciple. Before He instructed His disciples to follow Him in obedience, He told them they had to deny self. What does this mean to you?

One cannot walk out the Christian life without first denying self. In other words, we must disown the old way of doing and being in order to grab a hold of the new. The problem is we want to bring some aspects of our old life from the past into the present to justify it activities, as well as try to maintain the false dignity of it that will continually prove to be useless and a waste. I must stress that there is nothing of the old that can benefit our new life in Christ.

Jesus was clear, we must deny the right of self to maintain the old selfish life, and pick up the cross in order to follow Him. The old will defile the new, as well as prevent the work of cross from daily putting down the selfish dictates of the self-life. Obviously, the yoke of the cross is necessary if we are going to properly discipline how we are to walk out the new life *(Matthew 9:16-17; 16:24-25)*. It is important to point out that without self-denial the old man will simply become a noble martyr when the person applies the cross. He will appear noble, rehabilitated, and religious, when in fact nothing has changed about the inward disposition.

Jesus' desire is to lead us to a complete life. This life is satisfying and full. Such a life will stipulate us as His true disciple *(John 8:31-36; 10:10; 13:34-35; 15:7-14)*. There are requirements in being a disciple of Jesus. A true follower of Jesus will abide in Him, love others, obey His commands, and will display the fruit of heaven.

Self-denial is also a form of consecration *(Romans 12:1-2)*. "Consecration" means I am setting myself apart from all that is not of God, so that I can be sanctified or set apart unto God for His purpose and glory. Once I begin to consecrate my life in obedience to the Word of God, the Holy Spirit then begins the work of sanctification within *(1 Peter 1:2)*. As I walk in this sanctification, I become more consecrated in my disposition and lifestyle.

The Leading
of the Holy Spirit

Romans 8:1 tells us that those who walk after the Holy Spirit will not be condemned. What does it mean to walk after the Spirit and/or to be led by the Spirit? Walking after the Spirit involves faith and obedience. It is at the point of such faith that it is accounted for righteousness to us. Such righteousness will bring us under the leading of the Spirit *(Romans 8:14; Galatians 5:16-18)*. The more we give way to the Spirit in our walk, the more our lives are established in the wisdom, righteousness, sanctification, and redemption of Jesus Christ *(1 Corinthians 1:30)*.

Walking in the Spirit mortifies the works of the flesh. The Spirit also leads us into all truth about Jesus and into an intimate relationship with the Father as children of God. It is in this relationship we experience true communion *(John 16:13-14; Romans 8:13-17; 2 Corinthians 13:14)*.

Communion with God lies at the core of why Jesus came. He came to restore communion between God and man. It is in the Spirit that the fullness of the life of God is realized in us.

The Holy Spirit is both a gift and promise of the Father *(Luke 24:49; Acts 1:4; 2:38)* Jesus made this statement in *Luke 11:13*, *"If ye then, being evil, know how to give good gifts unto your children, how much more shall your heavenly Father give the Holy Spirit to them that ask him?"* Do we want more of God? Have you asked Him for more of His life, presence and working in Your life? We must discern if our inward environment is upright, and then we need to ask for more of God. He in turn will give us more of His Spirit. However, we must come to Him seeking more of His life.

Jesus confirmed this when this invitation went out to all who would come to receive, *"If any man thirst, let him come unto me, and drink. He that believeth on me, as the scripture hath said,*

112

out of his belly shall flow rivers of living water. (But this spoke he of the Spirit…") (John 7:37b-39a).

As you can see, faith is the means by which God delivers us from the consequences of sin. Denying self and application of the cross is God way of delivering us from the works of the flesh. The leading of the Holy Spirit is the way God delivers us from the condemnation of the world, as the Spirit leads us away from the influence of its far-reaching tentacle God's salvation is complete, but are we willing to receive it in its fullness or do we pick and choose what we will receive. The reason we pick and choose it is because we can hold on to certain aspects of the flesh and the world. The fruits will eventually reveal the choice of our heart. What does your fruit reveal about your life before God?

In Conclusion

We have only briefly touched on the issue of salvation. However, it is clear that we must receive by faith the Gospel as a heart revelation. In the Gospel we discover the light of this world. The light of the world is the life of Christ in the believer *(John 1:4; 2 Corinthians 4:3-6)*. We can initially accept the message intellectually, but if we fail to possess the Jesus of the Bible in our hearts, we will maintain our ignorance about God and ultimately taste His wrath.

Salvation will also be obvious in our lives. Granted, there may be various battles and some defeats, but if we are truly walking in our deliverance in obedience to the Word and according to the leading of the Holy Spirit, the light of the world (Jesus) will be reflected in and through our disposition *(2 Corinthians 3:18)*.

The question is do we have the witness of salvation in our lives? We must not consider this issue in any other light than the Word of God. We must not leave this up to religion, worldly philosophies, or the words of men.

Clearly in the present religious environment, the Gospel has been replaced with a feel-good religion that is akin to new-age philosophies and the humanistic religion where man's happiness is subtly being exalted in accordance to his feelings, desires, and pursuits *(Colossians 2:8)*. Needless to say, the Gospel and Christianity are being presented as a man-centered religion where man is being esteemed, reducing God to an entity that must come into subjection to man's fleshly whims and beliefs.

Sin has been downplayed with acceptable terms so that Christianity does not appear too legalistic and unloving. Moral accountability has been replaced with tolerance in the name of being politically correct, and the love of God has been repackaged to mean a fleshly love that walks in ignorance. Such love is more concerned with popular opinion and fleshly preference than it is to see men saved from their wretched condition.

Our challenge remains the same. We must find Christ in the midst of man's religion, worldly influences, heretical teachings, and demonic seduction and activities. We must seek out the true God for ourselves. We must answer the question concerning salvation for ourselves. As the Word declares, if we are saved, there will be a witness in our spirit that we have been delivered from the kingdom of Satan, and translated into the kingdom of God's dear Son *(Colossians 1:12-14)*.

Have you allowed such deliverance to take place in your life? Are you reflecting the disposition of Jesus or the disposition of the old man? Is there a deep abiding witness that you are indeed saved because Jesus lives in you by faith? Only you can answer these questions as you humbly bow before the Lord of lords and King of kings and seek His face about this most important matter.

Section 4

CHURCH AND LEADERSHIP

THE MAKEUP OF THE TRUE CHURCH

One of the most confusing issues about Christianity is what constitutes the Church of Jesus Christ. This question must be properly answered in order for people to understand what part fellowship, leadership, submission, and obedience play in the workings of the Body of Christ. What constitutes the real Church of Jesus to you?

To put the concept of church into perspective, a very simple question must be considered. Whom did Jesus die for? Did He die for a denomination, a certain group of people, a creed, or rituals? The right answer to this question will reveal the identity of the true Church of Jesus Christ whom He offered up His life on its behalf. The reason for this question is that Jesus loves His Church. However, the Church will be cleansed by the Word, and one day it will be presented to Him in a holy state, without spot, wrinkle, and blemish *(Ephesians 5:25-27)*.

Most of us probably know the correct answer to this question, but the word "church" has been used in such a way that there is much confusion about it. Most people relate to it as being a building, religious system, a certain denomination, or group of people. However, the Word of God is quite clear as to what constitutes the real Church that Jesus died for.

Colossians 1:18 tells us that the Church is made up of the Body of believers. In other words, those who have believed the Gospel of Jesus Christ. Such believers include those of the past, present, and future. According to *Hebrews 12:1,* there is a great cloud of witnesses who not only speaks of those of the Old Testament who possessed enduring faith, but confirms the power and expectation of this living, eternal Body to those of this present age. Therefore, religious association, denomination, leadership, and rituals do not constitute the Church.

Even though many people may be involved with Christian associations (parents/relatives/leaders or even terms such as Christian), certain Christian denominations, popular Christian leaders, and practicing regimented, religious rituals, do not make such people part of the true Church of Jesus. What has always made a person part of the Church and continues to identify this individual to this glorious Body is faith in the Person and redemptive work of the Lord Jesus Christ.

As you consider the attitudes of religious people, you will realize that many are displaying a cult mentality. We have been dealing with how a cult mentality is established, but now we need to understand what constitutes how this mentality expresses itself.

A cult mentality causes people to see their belief system, denomination, leaders, or practices as making them elite or superior to others in the Christian realm. They will often maintain they know the "right" truth and even have a corner on it. They may tolerate others, but they will be judgmental towards anything that is contrary to their belief system, leader, or practices. This is nothing more than self-righteousness.

Such elitism is prideful, and will delude and isolate these individuals from truth while causing schisms among them and other believers. Even though believers can be divided by certain beliefs, the true Body of Christ cannot be separated into different parts or pieces. It will always remain intact.

Religious foundations that are not founded on the Jesus of the Bible will not withstand the fiery trials of life. However, how many people assume they are saved because of their religious beliefs, affiliations, and practices? It is easy to fall into this category when your perception of spiritual matters is limited or wrong.

There is no elitism in the Body of Christ. In fact, those who are considered of less importance in the function of the Body of believers by the standards of the world, are actually exalted so that all will stand equally important before Jesus Christ who is the head of the Body *(1 Corinthians 12:12-27)*. Distribution of gifts among believers is not based on the talents, financial stability, importance, or outward appearances of people, but according to the working of the Holy Ghost for the purpose of the edification (or profit) of the whole Body *(1 Corinthians 12:4-11)*.

This brings us down to what the real Church of Jesus is. It is truly a living organism made up of believers. *1 Corinthians 3:9* tells us it is God's building. In other words, He resides in it. *1 Peter 2:5* calls believers lively stones that make up a spiritual house, a holy priesthood, establishing that the Church is the corporate body of Christ. Within this house, spiritual sacrifices are being offered that are acceptable to God by Jesus Christ. The apostle goes on to state this royal priesthood is a chosen generation, a peculiar (special) people who will show forth the praises for the One who has called them out of darkness into the marvelous light *(1 Peter 2:9)*.

Obviously, the real Church of Jesus walks according to the light or life of Jesus in it, and not according to the world or the flesh. This is why the Church is also considered a cultivated field *(1 Corinthians 3:9)*.

Clearly, God does the work within the hearts and lives of people that will bring forth eternal fruits. The people that make up this building and cultivated field of God will stand distinct from the world by their attitude, life, and fruits *(John 15:7-8; Ephesians 5:1-17)*.

How is this building established? The Word of God tells us one stone (believer) at a time. *1 Corinthians 12:13* tells us that each believer is baptized into this Body by the Holy Spirit.

Therefore, God places believers in this building according to His eternal purpose for each person's life, but it will always be in line with His plan for the whole Body of Christ.

This Body is to serve as an extension of Jesus in this present world *(1 Corinthians 12:18)*. No believer is an island unto themself. God's plan for each believer was ordained before the very foundation of the world. This body is also eternal and encompasses the world. As separate stones within the living, universal Church, we may not see our importance in the function of the whole Body of Christ, but we can know it is vital and significant in light of eternity.

Now that we understand how the Body is comprised, we need to come to terms with the leadership of this Body. The character of the Church will be based greatly on the leadership that is influencing it. Some of the Body of Christ is being rendered ineffective by improper leadership. It is important we gain the mind of Christ about this subject.

True Leadership

Explain how you perceive true leadership in the kingdom of God. *Ephesians 4:11* tells us that He gave some apostles, some prophets, some evangelists, some pastors, and some teachers. Do these people constitute leadership in the Church? To answer that question we must understand the distinct responsibility that they were given. As you will discover, true leaders in God's kingdom are not being called to a place of exaltation, but to a place of subjection and submission to the plan of God in relationship to the Church.

Leadership in the kingdom of heaven is different from the leadership promoted by the world. Jesus clearly brought this up in *Matthew 20:25-27,*

> *...Ye know that the princes of the Gentiles exercise dominion over them, and they that are great exercise*

authority over them. But it shall not be so among you, but whosoever will be great among you, let him be your minister, and whosoever will be chief among you, let him be your servant.

What can we learn about great leadership in God's kingdom? Simply put, God never calls His people to greater leadership, but to greater servitude.

A great leader in God's kingdom is not marked by titles, degrees, or places of great authority, but by a humble attitude of servitude before God that is clearly displayed towards His sheep. Jesus did not tell Peter, go forth, and my sheep will feed you. He commanded Peter to feed His lambs (new converts), and to feed His sheep (more mature believers), thereby, feeding His whole flock *(John 21:15-17)* Jesus also clearly left us an example of servitude the night He was betrayed *(Matthew 20:28; John 13:13-17)*

As you study these five positions mentioned in Ephesians, you will realize they must come into subjection to the Cornerstone, Jesus Christ, as a means to ensure every believer is firmly planted on the foundation of Jesus. *Ephesians 2:19-22* confirms this,

Now, therefore, ye are no more strangers and foreigners, but fellow citizens with the saints, and of the household of God: And are built upon the foundation of the apostles and prophets, Jesus Christ himself being the chief corner stone, In whom all the building fitly framed together groweth unto an holy temple in the Lord; In whom ye also are built together for an habitation of God through the Spirit.

We already know the foundation has been clearly established by the apostles and prophets in their writings. There is only one spiritual foundation and that is Jesus Christ *(1 Corinthians 3:11)*. There is nothing more to establish about this foundation. The building or temple (His people) is now being brought forth, but it is in line with the Cornerstone, Jesus.

According to the information I have read on cornerstones, all other stones are lined up to the cornerstone. Therefore, what we need to understand is that the work of the apostles and prophets are to ensure that the Church is lining up to the Person, work, teachings, and examples of Jesus Christ. The problem today is that many of the so-called "leaders" of the Church are redefining the foundation in order to exalt themselves into the place of Jesus Christ as the cornerstone.

Today there is a flood of so-called "apostles" and "prophets" running around. In fact, leaders are flattering and appealing to people's pride as these unsuspecting individuals are given titles of importance in these leaders' "spiritual kingdoms." As a result, many are being seduced by doctrines of demons *(Ephesians 5:6-7; 1 Timothy 4:1-2)*.

There are innumerable people running around with new revelations as well as a word here and a word there because they call themselves apostles or prophets. However, if you study about the true apostles and prophets in the Word of God, they were a rare breed.

They were not of this world. They stood distinct and they were not looking for followers. Their uncompromising attitudes brought persecution upon them. They spoke the oracles of God, which cut through the religious kingdoms of men. They were not popular or appreciated because they never fit into the popular religious systems or movements of their day. As you can imagine, this study would take many volumes to do it any real justice.

The goal of this exposition is to bring godly leadership in the proper perspective. True leaders in the kingdom of God will establish people firmly on the Jesus of the Bible, and ensure they are lining up to Him as the Cornerstone. As Jesus stated, those who obey and teach men to observe the commandments of God will be great, but those who fail to obey God's commandments, and likewise teach others to disobey will be considered the least in His kingdom *(Matthew 5:19)*.

As you consider **apostles**, they were sent forth to establish local bodies of believers. In the case of **prophets**, they were watchmen who were to warn, guard, and exhort God's people in regard to truth. Their goal was to always point people towards the reality of God in their midst. They would warn against anything that would threaten that reality, and they would guard the truth against the invasion of idolatry, heresy, and evil works, knowing that it was the only means to bring proper contrast. They would exhort God's people to believe, obey, and walk according to His righteous ways.

Evangelists are responsible to stir up the vision of God's people. Once God's people lose their vision for the lost, they will lose sight of their calling and responsibility towards God to fulfill His plan to bring forth a complete revelation of the Son. Evangelists have the calling and ability to once again stir up that vision. This means that God's people will be awakened from the sleep of complacency, the dullness of compromise, and to be stirred up by the quickening of the Holy Spirit to consider the holy. They will once again gain the passion of love for God, as well as be set aflame with that which inspires them to fulfill His will.

Pastors are the shepherds of the flock. Their main goal is to ensure that the sheep are properly following Jesus. These people may be good preachers or teachers or both, but this does not distinguish them as real pastors. Real pastors possess the heart of Jesus towards His flock.

They protect the sheep from wolves, they stand against the infiltration of muddy (heretical) waters, and they know how to bind up the wounds of the sheep. They are the truest example of servants to the sheep, and their goal is to see the sheep mature in their relationship with the one true Shepherd who gave His life for them.

Apostles appeal to the spiritual needs of people, while prophets appeal to the spiritual condition of people, evangelists appeal to the vision of people, and shepherds appeal to the heart of people, but **teachers** appeal to the understanding of people. The greatest teachers do not tell people how to think; rather they give them the tools that will challenge their way of thinking. Great teachers want to enlarge people's ability to consider the possibilities of a matter. It is not just a matter of enlarging their ability to explore outside of the normal, intellectual boxes that many operate within, but it is about enlarging one's world concerning a matter. This is why the Holy Spirit is the real teacher of the saint. He enables, instructs, enlarges, and leads a person to the truth about the impossible, the incredible, and the eternal *(John 16:13; 1 John 2:27)*.

The responsibilities of apostles, prophets and evangelists may change according to the needs and growth of the Church. In other words, these positions will not remain constant in the local Body. Apostles and prophets may be sent elsewhere or placed in different types of leadership positions. The evangelist must move to different harvest fields. However, the positions of pastor and teachers remain constant and necessary in local bodies.

This brings us to the real leadership of local bodies. The Word of God clearly stipulates there are two such positions in the local churches. They are **elders** and **deacons**. The Apostle Paul clearly establishes the criteria of these two leadership positions.

Elders are overseers. They oversee the well-being and spiritual growth of the Body. Elders are also called bishops and presbyters. Pastors are also considered elders. We get a sense of elders in *Acts 6*.

There was a conflict in the new Church. Those who were overseeing (elders) the Church felt they needed to give themselves to prayer and the ministry of the Word of God to avoid being spread out too thin, thereby, neglecting their duties *(Acts 6:4)*. In *1 Timothy 3* and *Titus 1*, you can read about the character and duties of an elder. Here are just a few qualifications of an elder.

These leaders must be sober-minded, of good behavior, given to hospitality, and apt to teach. They must not display obsessive behavior, and they must know how to properly rule their own house. Such leaders must be able to exhort and convince with sound doctrine those who oppose truth. They must be a steward of God, and not self-willed.

The word "deacon" means minister or servant. These are the people who minister to the practical needs of the local Body. This is also brought out in *Acts 6*. One of the men who stepped into this position as a minister of the Body was the first martyr of the Church, Stephen. It is said of Stephen that he was full of faith and of the Holy Spirit.

Although Stephen was ministering to the practical needs of the local body, it was obvious that to be effective in ministering, a deacon must be led by the Spirit and walk by faith. The criteria of deacons reveal character that would maintain the trust of those they minister too. For example, they could not be double-tongued, they had to be true to their word and discreet about what they said or shared about a matter. They had to be sober-minded, faithful in all things, and bold in their faith. Such a person would also have one spouse, and had to properly rule their house *(1 Timothy 3:8-13)*.

Today there are people who hold the positions of elders and deacons, but how many fit the qualifications? Many of these people hold these positions because of gifts, associations, or financial status, but not because they fit the qualifications.

Elders and deacons make up boards that are often subject to a particular hierarchy (such as the pastor) and deal with financial strategies in order to keep the church doors open to do business as usual. However, these people do not really oversee the well-being or practical needs of the sheep.

Since the integrity of the real leadership of the Church has become compromised by wrong attitudes towards what was clearly set forth in the Word of God, the local churches do not have the necessary strength that comes from godly leadership. When you compromise the integrity of any leadership, the authority will be missing. Without the authority, there is no real protection, causing the local body to become prey to wolves and hireling shepherds.

Clearly, the local body needs to come back to center as to the type of leadership that was designated by God. Men and women who fit the criteria must be put in their perspective places to ensure the health and safety of local churches. For such people, it will not be a matter of prestige, money, or means, but of character, calling, heart, and vision. True leaders do not drive, demand, or torment the sheep; rather they lead in humility and serve as an example, while challenging the sheep in meekness, exhorting them in love, and proving to be long-suffering in instruction.

This gives a summary of true leadership in the kingdom of God. We desperately need to establish godly leadership. Local bodies have become weak and are falling prey to heresies, wolves, and hireling shepherds that couldn't care less about the sheep, but see their position as the means to feed themselves and exalt themselves before men. As a result, they scatter the sheep, which will ultimately bring destruction to God's flock *(Isaiah 56:10-12; Jeremiah 23:1-3; 50:6; Ezekiel 34:2-3* refer to *Zechariah 11:17)*. However, abuse of the sheep means greater damnation for these false shepherds.

It is the responsibility of the sheep to seek out the true shepherds. After all, the shepherd is only as good as the sheep and the sheep are only as good as the shepherd. Sheep can complain about their shepherd, but many of the sheep are feeding in the pastures that serve their personal preferences. Sheep must take responsibility for their own spiritual welfare, keep their eyes on the true Shepherd, Jesus Christ, and remain sensitive to the leading of His voice.

Ordinances of the Church

The Church has been given ordinances to observe. Without reading any further, test your understanding of this matter. How many ordinances have been given to the Church, what are they, and who gave them to the Body of Believers?

Jesus gave the Church two ordinances to recognize and practice. Sadly, the practices of these two ordinances are controversial even in the Body of Believers. How important is it for believers to have the right perspective about these decrees?

"Ordinance" means a practice or ceremony that has been ordained. Something that is ordained has an authoritative decree or direction behind it. Jesus not only ordained these two ordinances, He practiced them, leaving us an example for both of them.

The first ordinance was established at the beginning of His ministry. It is that of water baptism. When John the Baptist was reluctant to baptize Jesus, He made this statement in *Matthew 3:15, "Suffer it to be so now, for thus it becometh us to fulfill all righteousness."* The initial purpose for water baptism was for the remission of sins *(Mark 1:4)*. However, Jesus was without sin; therefore, His baptism represented an act of righteousness.

As Christians, how should we look at baptism, and what should the proper procedure be surrounding this ceremony? There are two reasons behind water baptism: identification and righteousness.

A person who is baptized does so as a means of becoming identified with Jesus' death, burial, and resurrection. It is a visible witness and sign of the new life. *Romans 6:3-5* tells us as believers that we have been baptized into Jesus, thereby, we were baptized into His death. Such a baptism allows us to be raised up in newness of life. We are also told that believers are baptized into one Body by the Holy Ghost *(1 Corinthians 12:12-13).*

Water baptism is also an upright act because it was a commandment given by Jesus to His disciples before He ascended to heaven,

> *All power is given unto me in heaven and in earth. Go ye, therefore, and teach all nations, baptizing them in the name or the Father, and of the Son, and of the Holy Ghost, teaching them to observe all things whatsoever I have commanded you; and lo, I am with you always, even unto the end of the world (Matthew 28:18-20).*

You would think that the issue of water baptism would not be controversial, but it is. You have infant baptism that "supposedly" ensures that the original sin is addressed, as well as baptism for the dead. These acts of baptism would imply that baptism is part of salvation. In fact, there are those who believe it is a requirement for salvation.

As you study Scripture, there is only one mention of baptism for the dead in *1 Corinthians 15:29.* Examination of this Scripture shows it was in relationship to a pagan practice. Paul was using it as an example to show that even certain pagan beliefs recognize that there would be the resurrection of the dead.

There is no Scripture supporting infant baptism. Children were dedicated to the Lord such as the prophet Samuel, but there is no indication that infants were baptized to ensure their spiritual protection or well-being *(1 Samuel 1:11; 2:11).* For example, God stated about the pending death of the infant son of wicked King Jeroboam that He had found some good thing towards him in the child *(1 Kings 14:12-13).* David did not baptize his infant child, knowing that the child would not survive. Yet, he was assured of seeing his child in the next life, even though the child represented an adulterous act between him and Bathsheba *(2 Samuel 12:13-23).*

When it comes to maintaining that a person must be baptized to ensure salvation, *Mark 16:16* does not confirm such a belief. Granted, people are to be baptized out of an act of identification and righteousness, which is a matter of faith or believing something to be true and upright. However, what will solely cause people to perish in their sins is not believing the Gospel message.

The thief on the cross brings out such a concept. He could not come down from the cross to be baptized, but he believed and was assured of being with Jesus in Paradise *(Luke 23:39-43).* This brings us to the promotion of another Gospel, meaning Jesus plus some type of work or practice such as water baptism.

Jesus alone saves, and the Word of God is clear, we are saved by grace and not by any personal merits or works. Once again, we are reminded that true salvation will be accompanied by works or acts of righteousness *(Ephesians 2:8-10; Hebrews 6:9).*

There are different ways of baptizing. Some sprinkle water, while others submerge the person into water. Is there a right way and a wrong way? For many it is a subject you dare not touch without incurring tremendous debate or passion and wrath. It is vital to consider how God does something. He never does it part way. For example, Jesus, who is God, became total man in every way, except He was without sin. He was completely submerged into the human race. With this in mind, must we accept symbols and practices that are not complete in their identification or representation? Do we dare believe God would support such practices?

When you consider the word "baptism" in the *Strong's Exhaustive Concordance,* it comes from a Greek word, "baptizo" which means to be fully wet or completely submerged *(# 907-911).* Do we ignore the meaning of words to maintain the practices taught to us by family or denominational preference? The issue is the same. It does not matter what man's conclusions may be to an issue. Rather, how does the Word of God address the issue in teaching and example?

There is also the matter of what words are used at the baptism. There are those who baptize in the name of the Father, the Son, and the Holy Ghost. There are also those who baptize in the name of Jesus only. We have both examples in Scripture *(Matthew 28:19; Acts 8:16; 10:48)*. Are there inconsistencies between these two instructions? Once again, is there a right way or wrong way? If there is confusion, what is the safest route to take in such matters?

In Matthew, Jesus, our Lord, is giving the instruction as to how to baptize. What must come into submission? Should we bring Jesus' words into submission to examples found in *Acts*, or should we bring all matters into submission to Jesus' words?

People must remember that Jesus represents the fullness of the deity in bodily form *(Colossians 2:9)*. God the Father and the Holy Spirit were unveiled in the Old Testament. However, Jesus was a mystery until He was revealed in the New Testament. By instructing Jesus' followers to baptize in His name, was it their way of ensuring that baptism would be a completed ordinance by pointing to the Person of Jesus Christ as well? After all, in bodily form He represents the fullness of the Godhead, the Father and the Holy Ghost. Did the people realize that the fullness of the Father and the Holy Ghost were being completely represented in the Person of Jesus when they were baptized in His name?

Acts 10:48, uses the term "Lord". Lord points to Adonai, which points to "owner." Once again, are all three persons of the Godhead being represented in this term? It is important to consider that when the man Jesus was baptized, the Holy Ghost came down in the form of a dove and the Father made His presence known by introducing His Son. Can we deduct from this example that all three must be recognized as being a vital part of our identification to Jesus and His redemption? In a way Jesus verified this when He commanded His followers to baptize in the name of the Father, the Son, and the Holy Ghost. Keep in mind, Jesus is the one who serves as our example and Master. He did things according to "righteousness," and we are to walk as He walked (*1 John 2:6*).

When it comes to the ordinance of "Communion," there is also disagreement. What is your understanding of this ordinance?

Water baptism signified the beginning of Jesus' ministry. However, "Communion" signals the end of Jesus' mission on earth. Notice the terms used. Jesus' ministry continues in the courts of heaven. He serves as our High Priest, Mediator, and Advocate. However, His earthly mission was to die for us as God's Passover Lamb. On the night He was betrayed He shared "Communion" as His last act with His disciples before He was offered up as the Lamb of God.

The debates over Communion vary from the type of emblems used right down to its meaning. Some people believe that unleavened bread and wine (grape juice) should be used, signifying that Jesus was without sin; therefore, He stood as a sacrifice without blemish (or leaven) (*1 Corinthians 5:6-8*). Some people believe any old bread or drink, such as water, can be used. Some insist on wine and wafers. Who is right? Can any old emblems do, or should we insist on the purity of the emblems that will not only uphold the meaning of what each one represents, while maintaining the spirit or intent of the ordinance?

The meaning behind this ordinance varies as well. For some people, to partake of communion means they are literally partaking of the actual body and blood of Jesus. For others, the bread and wine are nothing more than symbols that remind them of what Jesus accomplished the night He partook of this ceremony with His disciples. Who is right and who is wrong? Is it important we get it right? For some, it is a matter of salvation.

Is it possible to actually eat of the body and drink the blood of Jesus? Jesus made reference to this concept in *John 6:53-58.* He stated that if you did not eat of His body and drink of His blood, you could not possess eternal life. However, does this mean it is something that can be done literally?

It is important to realize that this proved to be a hard saying to many of His disciples. They turned away from Him and followed Him no more *(John 6:60-66).* Why were they offended? I believe they were taking it literally as well. However, Jesus clearly explained what He meant.

In *John 6:32-35,* Jesus was speaking of Himself as the Bread of life that came down from heaven. He makes this statement in *John 6:40, "And this is the will of him that sent me, that everyone who seeth the Son, and believeth on him, may have everlasting life; and I will raise him up at the last day."*

Believing is brought up at different points in this chapter. Was Jesus simply telling people that if they believe in Him, it would be the same as partaking of His body and drinking of His blood, which points to identification? If this is the correct perspective, it would make more sense than believing that one must literally partake of His body and drink His blood to be saved. If you think about each perspective, both require some type of faith. Obviously, those who believe that they are literally partaking of His body and blood must have the faith to believe that each time they partake of the emblems from the hands of their leaders, these substances are actually turned into the body and blood of Jesus.

Perhaps *John 6:57* will bring more clarity to this matter: *"As the living Father hath sent me, and I live by the Father, so he that eateth me, even he shall live by me."* When you consider the concept of "live," it also points to walk. We know we do not walk by sight, but by faith *(2 Corinthians 5:7).*

With this in mind, consider *Galatians 2:20, I am crucified with Christ: nevertheless I live; yet not I but Christ liveth in me; and the life I now live in the flesh I live by the faith of the Son of God, who loved me and gave himself for me."* (Emphasis added.) Clearly, we have the life of Christ in us, and we live according to His life by faith *(Hebrews 10:37-39)*. Our life in Christ is clearly established by faith in all we do when it comes to loving Him and obeying His Word. Obedience is a type of assimilation of that life in our life.

On this basis what would make more sense? Let us now consider it from another perspective. Faith is practical, and not based on imagination or fanciful notions. When Jesus was conducting "Communion", He raised the bread and instructed His disciples that it was His body. He did the same with the wine. He declared it was His blood *(Luke 22:14-20)*. Was He saying, "Imagine that these two emblems are my body and blood?"

It is important to point out that faith does not work off the basis of imagination, and just because we imagine something, does not make it reality. Would Jesus say that it was His literal body and blood, when in fact it was clear to all present it was not?

The key is found in why they would eat of the bread and drink of the wine—it was in remembrance of Him. Remembrance is a memorial as to a person or event. From this example, are we to conclude that these emblems symbolize Jesus' broken body and shed blood in order to remind us of what He accomplished on the cross?

Those who partake of the ritual of Communion according to Paul's instruction consider the present, the past, and future. For example, each person must examine themself before taking of the emblems to see if they are presently prepared to take of Communion in a worthy manner *(1 Corinthians 11:28)*. From the basis of preparation, people take of the bread reminding them that Jesus' stripes heal them *(1 Peter 2:24)*. They take of the wine, remembering that it is by His blood that their redemption was acquired *(Hebrews 9:15-22)*.

Each time Christians partake of Communion, they are declaring that Jesus is coming again *(1 Corinthians 11:26)* Communion may be a time to consider our present condition, and remember our spiritual heritage, but it also points to a glorious future. Jesus said it best the night He was sharing this time with His disciples.

> *And he said unto them, With desire I have desired to eat this Passover with you before I suffer. For I say unto you I will not any more eat of it, until it be fulfilled in the kingdom of God. And he took the cup, and gave thanks and said, Take this and divide it among yourselves; For I say unto you, I will not drink of the fruit of the vine, until the kingdom of God shall come (Luke 22:15-18).*

Scripture shows us that the kingdom of God would abide within the heart of man through Jesus Christ, but one day it will be fully realized in heaven at the marriage supper of the Lamb. The Lamb of God will sup with all of those who belong to Him. It will be a glorious celebration *(Revelation 19:7-9)*.

There should not be any debate about these two ordinances, but there is. You must wonder why there is such a debate. It is simple; man's interpretations and traditions have confused the meanings and practices behind these two ordinances. If we would strip away all man's influences and indoctrination that put all the different twists on Scripture, and simply believe what is written, there would be no debate about matters. It would be clear in its simplicity and easy to respond to in spirit and in righteousness.

Do you have inward debates going on in your soul about these two ordinances? Do not let man, religious traditions, or theology settle them for you. Allow the Word to settle it by believing what it says. Do not make more of a matter by spiritualizing it to mean something it does not mean, but do not strip it of its spirit by failing to gain God's perspective. Seek God's perspective about a matter so that the things of God can be fulfilled in your life in the right spirit and in truth. Such completion will result in peace with God, satisfaction of the soul, and rest to the mind.

Benevolence

One of the main goals behind a cult is not only to spread their erroneous message, but also to gain control of the hearts and minds of people so that they can control their finances. The goal of cult leaders is the same; they are after money as a means of supporting and promoting their so-called "self-serving gospels and kingdoms."

What is your understanding concerning the subject of giving in the kingdom of God?

The main concept many shepherds use to shake the money out of their people is that of tithing. However, if you study tithing it was for the Levitical priesthood and for the upkeep of the temple. Since there is no temple in Jerusalem and the Priesthood is not in place, the Jewish people do not pay tithes. After all, tithes had to do with the Law in regards to the increase of land (crops) and animals. These tithes were used for sacrifices and celebrations, as well as set apart as food for the priests *(Leviticus 27:30-32; Numbers 18:21, 31:9, 27-29)*.

It is important to point out that I have nothing against people paying 1/10th of their income to those who watch over their souls, but my problem rests with the fact that many religious leaders use the term "tithes" to forced people to give to the kingdom they are promoting. This is not only unscriptural, but it is not a New Testament practice. The New Testament practice is that of being a good steward of what God has entrusted. The Apostle Paul talks about Christian giving in *2 Corinthians 9*.

The first aspect of giving Paul brings up is the principle behind giving, "But this I say, He who soweth sparingly shall reap also sparingly; and he who soweth bountifully shall reap also bountifully" *(2 Corinthians 9:6)*. People give for different reasons, but few give for the right reason. Everything belongs to God and everything must be offered back to Him for His use to ensure good and faithful stewardship on the part of His servants. It is only as we offer all back as His servants that it will go through the hands of God. Once it goes through His hands He can bless, sanctify, and multiply it for His glory *(Luke 9:13-17; 2 Corinthians 9:10-11)*.

The second part of godly giving is the right attitude. Giving is a form of ministry. God made this statement in *Deuteronomy 28:47-48a, "Because thou servedst not the LORD thy God with joyfulness, and with gladness of heart, for the abundance of all things; therefore shalt thou serve thine enemies which the LORD shall send against thee."* People give out of duty, out of conscience, and out of show. Such people are giving out of religious pressure, guilt, and for self-exaltation. However, godly giving that will bring pleasure and honor to God is giving that comes out of a heart that is upright towards God, and is cheerful in its service before Him *(2 Corinthians 9:7)*.

The third aspect of godly giving is that it serves as a sacrifice. *2 Corinthians 9:8* talks about how godly giving is a type of good work. *Hebrews 13:15-16* talks about how good works are considered a type of sacrifice to God. God desires to abound in His grace towards every good work. Again, God is able to bless, sanctify, and multiply every good work for His use and glory.

Since we are talking about sacrifice, there are three types of sacrifices when it comes to our giving. The first type of sacrifice is the **religious sacrifice**. We give that which will satisfy our religious conscience. It has nothing to do with stewardship, but with that of duty. Such giving represents the least we can do to keep religion and God off of our backs.

The second sacrifice is our **reasonable service** *(Romans 12:1)*. In other words, it is a matter of doing what is right before God. Such righteousness is not a matter of sacrifice, but one of reasonable service, but it will fall into the category of good works that God is able to use for His glory.

The final sacrifice is the one that **comes out of our need** and not out of abundance or what is considered reasonable. Sacrifices that come out of need cannot be confused with that which we do out of impulsiveness. Impulsiveness proves to be the product of our carnal emotions and foolishness. The real issue behind acceptable sacrifice is not the quantity of it; rather, it is the quality. God does not need our sacrifices, but He desires actions that show our good faith towards Him.

A good example of the type of sacrifice that comes out of our need is the widow and her mites in *Mark 12:41-44*. The widow's two mites may have seemed insignificant to the world's way of looking, but God took note of her giving and used it as an example to others. This widow gave out of her lack by faith in God. This is the type of sacrifice that God deserves from each of us, and desires to see. It is a sacrifice of the heart that gives sacrificially in good faith to a God who is trustworthy in every way.

Godly giving will manifest itself in liberal giving *(2 Corinthians 9:13)*. The reason for this is due to benevolence. Our God is a God of benevolence. His desire is to bring good will or kindness. We should manifest this same benevolence due to the fact we actually owe others good will or kindness. Such good will and kindness are because of what Jesus did on the cross. We have been bought with a price and we owe all to our Master, Lord, Savior, and God. Jesus brought this out when He gave His followers a third commandment in *1 John 13:34-35, "A new commandment I give unto you, that ye love one another; as I have loved you, that ye also love one another. By this shall all men know that ye are my disciples, if ye have love one to another."*

Jesus gave His best, He gave His all, and He gave it on our behalf. His sacrifice showed the good will and kindness of God towards humanity. As believers, can we do any less when it comes to those who are part of the Body of Jesus? Paul said it best when he gave this instruction in *Galatians 6:2, "Bear ye one another's burdens, and so fulfill the law of Christ."*

The problem with the subject of giving is that many members of cults gave it all out of religious duty to only be betrayed. As they look back, the idea of the waste of time, energy, and resources can be overwhelming. They can look back and see how they often sacrificed the well-being of their family, as well as themselves. As they look at the emptiness, the lies, and the deception of it all, they must do all they can to fight back the anger and bitterness that can erupt like a volcano, spilling out despair in their souls. They must make sure they do not become a victim a second time to bitterness. This would mean they once again come under the darkness and false world of Satan and his counterfeits.

Those coming out of cults must seek God to heal them and put all matters in perspective including their giving. In fact, God could have accepted such giving as a sweet sacrifice. After all, the widow put her mites into the coffers of a religious system that stood condemned *(Matthew 3:9-10)*. However, she was not giving it to the religious system, but to God. Once she gave it to God for His glory, it was no longer her concern, but those to whom she entrusted it.

It is vital we do not look back like Lot's wife on that which is already judged. We must go forward in our life with God by learning the lessons of the past to change the terrain of the present. By changing the present terrain of our life according to the Lord's good pleasure, we will be assured of the glorious future with Him.

Regarding my own situation, I have many different markers from the past that represent certain aspects of my life. At one time, those markers represented my terrible failures, but when I realized that they possessed valuable lessons that needed to be learned, they began to mark spiritual growth rather than past failures. In the process of changing my markers, I learned it is how you look at a matter. In God's economy, there are no failures or waste, just markers that mark a passing of an old life and the establishment of a new life.

Let us rejoice over the markers of the old life, knowing we will never have to pass by their way again, recognizing that such markers of the past now represent the maturity of our present character, clearly refined by experience resulting in change, and producing wisdom from above *(Romans 5:3-5)*.

Section 5

CONFRONTING
THE
CULT MENTALITY

EXPOSING THE
CULT MENTALITY

Most people are interested in what a cult is, but few are interested in how cults affect their victims. Cults establish what I call a cult mentality.

When I was first saved, I remember one of the concerns of those who were involved with me was, "She may have come out of the cult, but did the cult come out of her?" The first time I heard this statement, I was confused. What did they mean about the cult being out of me?

It took years before I realized what this statement means. When you consider what a cult is, you realize that it is a belief or teaching that often runs close to and parallel with what is true. In other words, it may sound like truth, it may look like truth, and it may feel like truth, but it is not truth. Obviously, cults can be exposed based on what they promote or present as truth.

However, it is not that easy to identify and confront the affects a cult has on people. You can identify something as being wrong, but the real battle is not at the point of something being wrong, rather the real battle comes down to the extent or level that such wrong has managed to influence the heart and mind of a person.

The heart will often display loyalty towards the cult or leader regardless of how it may be proven wrong. The mind has usually been influenced in such a way that when the foundation of a cult is proven wrong, such knowledge will be rendered useless because it cannot penetrate through the indoctrination that has been firmly set into place.

The battle for a person's soul does not rest on proving that a cult's belief system is wrong, rather the real battle rages over the blind loyalty and idolatrous affections that have enslaved these individuals into a darkness that will pervert the purity of the light when it is present. When people come out of a cult, the darkness of it will prevent these people from being properly challenged to know, seek out, and find the truth. The deadly seeds of deception and heresy will undermine any good seed. What many people fail to realize is that we learn our behavioral patterns according to our thinking and conduct by that which has influenced our lives *(Deuteronomy 18:9; Psalm 106:33-40; Proverbs 22:24-25).*

Those who have come under the spirit and indoctrination of a cult have been conditioned to reject truths that do not compliment or reinforce the teachings of the leader or creeds. Truth will seem foreign, offensive, and repulsive to such a person. Therefore, most people coming out from under the influences of a cult are already conditioned to walk in total rejection of any truth that is affiliated with true religion, as well as being susceptible to come under the spirit and influence of another counterfeit. In fact, such people will be naturally attracted to anything that will reject or oppose true religion.

For example, people who have been hurt by a cult already feel betrayed by religion. At this point, they are suspicious of everything. They do not trust the Word of God, because it has been improperly handled. Since they have been indoctrinated to see or interpret the Word from an erroneous point of view, truth will be perverted, preventing it from making the necessary impact. Due to their spiritual captivity, such people do not trust unfeigned leadership or the Word. They have no foundation in which to test anything. This leaves them judgmental, rather than discerning. On this basis, how does one test a matter? Since these people feel so miserable about what has happened to them, the greatest attraction will be to that which makes them feel good about self or life.

In ministering to such people, I have to keep in mind that they are fragile when it comes to religious matters. You never know what point of truth in the Word of God will set them off. They can become immediately insulted over a Scripture or teaching, and put up a wall. Since they feel bad, hurt, or betrayed, they will fight against, argue with, or reject the truth. It is a terrible state indeed. Rejection of the truth reveals that such people are not inclined towards the truth. They prove to be angry and rebellious about all religious matters. As a result, they walk in unbelief towards what is true. They end up rejecting the very thing that could set them free from their plight.

Just because something in the Word has been misused or improperly presented, does not make it any less truth. We are clearly told that we will be judged by the complete counsel of the Word of God. The Word of God will stand when all other philosophies, erroneous beliefs, and religious preferences are consumed in the fires of hell. Sadly, many of these people keep exchanging one empty, destructive religious package for another. As Jesus said, those who make converts or disciples out of their particular way of thinking, make such people two-fold the children of hell *(Matthew 23:15)*.

Another aspect about cults is that they use a lot of Christian platitudes and terminology. Sadly, Christianity has been reduced to a subculture within the American culture. We have our own language and way of doing things. However, very few Christians have a grasp on Christian terminology.

The reason for this gap is that many Christians assume people understand the meanings behind Christian terms. These assumptions have even caused people in leadership positions to be lax in teaching the correct meaning to ensure integrity and the right spirit behind the words or terms. As a result, people have been left to fill in the blanks. Even though there are fruits that indicate that words or terms hold different meanings for cults, it is not unusual for believers to assume that there is an agreement. However, cult members will associate words or terms to their particular cult's twisted presentation. When the correct presentation challenges these people's foundation it causes them to become closed or skeptical.

The other tactic that is used is platitudes. Platitudes are used when people do not know how to address a real issue or problem. These platitudes can be select Scriptures or what we would consider words of wisdom or popular terms. However, platitudes just reveal our ignorance and not our wisdom. They come across as indifferent, unfeeling, and judgmental. I cannot tell you how many times people have whipped platitudes on me to put me in my place, exalt their so-called "superior wisdom" or to get me off their back. Platitudes are nothing but bones people throw out as a distraction.

One might wonder how people fall into cults. We need to realize that cults are designed to be attractive to our pride, as well as our desire to experience a religious fantasy. These individuals are also religious enough that they appeal to our religious conscience. Let us consider how cults are geared to attract our pride.

One aspect of a cult is that it makes you feel elite. For example, a cult maintains it has a corner on truth and all other beliefs are wrong. This is elitism and it attracts our pride.

Being part of the elite causes people to feel superior over those who are part of what is considered mainline Christianity or the so-called "blind stupidity" of the ignorant religious masses. It is important to point out that there are no new truths, just greater revelations of the Jesus of the Bible. God has maintained that His Word is true. If anything proves to be contrary to the intent or teachings of His Word, it must be considered a lie from hell *(Romans 3:3-4)*. I might add that elitism is a tactic that Hitler used on a generation of people, and six million Jews died as a result.

Another area that attracts our pride is how cults use titles, prophecies, gifts, and positions. Cults leaders are notorious for handing out titles and positions to people they want to influence and control. Such people feel that the leader is seeing their worth and potential; therefore, they feel not only special but also obliged to follow that leader into hell itself.

Another area is that of spiritual gifts. These gifts are handed out like candy to the people. It goes like this: "You have the gift of healing." "You have a gift of prophecy." "Now that your gift has been identified, you need to operate in this gift among the people." At this point, the individual feels special, and has the promise of serving God.

They see this allotment as personal recognition and exaltation as well as the means to influence people. The problem with this presentation is that the Bible tells us the Holy Spirit gives gifts, as He wills, not as man delegates. A person may be used in a certain gift at different times, but they do not have a corner on the gift. Gifts are a sovereign manifestation of the Holy Spirit *(1 Corinthians 12:7-11)*. They are for the purpose of edification for the whole Body and not a matter of identification to the importance or personal exaltation of a person.

The problem with the misuse of gifts among people who have not been properly instructed in this matter is that religion becomes a matter of experience. This experience supersedes truth and becomes a fleshly, emotional wave that anyone can get caught up in when the flesh, not the Spirit, so moves them in their religious fervor to operate in their so-called "gifts."

The problem is escalated when these people take their positions or gifts seriously. In other words, they pride themselves on their position or gifts, and feel that they are in a leadership position because they are elite or special. When this pride reaches it pinnacle, it becomes superior. Due to the open door of pride, this person is now operating in a religious spirit or under an antichrist spirit.

Such people border on fanaticism about their mission, calling, gifts, or positions. They cannot handle present reality and resent anyone who would dare challenge them about their wrong spirit or belief. They prove to be unteachable; therefore, all they hear will be perverted and quickly rejected unless it feeds their religious fantasy.

The religious spirit demands attention, consideration, and exaltation. When the person who is motivated by such a spirit fails to get the desired recognition, they become angry and disillusioned with the church. Since this spirit must be recognized, the person will leave the local church in search of a religious platform that will honor them. Therefore, the heresy and spirit that is in operation in this individual is spread to the unsuspecting Body of Believers.

If the pastor is not strong in faith, Spirit-led and inspired, the leader will not be able to discern the cancer that is confronting the congregation. This cancer will cause a mixture (mixed spirit) or confusion. Ultimately, it can cause division.

Another means that is used involves fear and guilt. Cults know how to manipulate misguided devotion and trust. They cause people to rely on them for their spiritual direction and credibility. Approval from the cult leader and members of the cult becomes a necessary pursuit. Therefore, it is easy for cult leaders to classify questions about their teachings as rebellious. Opinions that differ outside of the cult leader's beliefs are considered independence or pride. To have a life outside of the "elite" group is to undermine the authority of the leader. Fear and guilt not only keeps the person operating in superstition about God, but it also can be effectively used by the cult leader to keep the person under control.

Cults also play with the emotions of their members through the avenues of a merit system. For example, keep the approval of the cult leader or organization at all cost, and all is well. Lose that approval, and fear of rejection or chastisement along with guilt will raise its head. Cult leaders effectively use fear and guilt to gain and maintain control of people.

145

The greatest obstacle when it comes to the cult mentality is the person's perception of God's Word. All cults present a different God, redefine Jesus, and undermine the authority of the Word of God. Since the cult mentality sets up a perverted perception of God and His Word, there is no standard that can be presented to these people that is able to bring them to a place of discernment and accountability. Without the standard, there is no means by which a person can come to terms about what they believe, know, or understand.

This brings me to my own struggles to ensure the cult mentality was no longer influencing my way of thinking or evaluating a matter. Although the cult I belonged to undermined the Word of God, I realized I had to choose it as a standard by which I would test all of my beliefs. In order to do this, I had to repent in three areas. "Repent" means I had to change my mind, thereby, changing my direction. As I changed my direction, I changed my focus. It was as I changed my focus that my mind began to be transformed, producing godly conduct.

The first area I had to repent in was for my choice as to what I considered my standard of truth. I had to recognize my cult was wrong, in error, and a genuine cult. I did not agree totally with the cult to which I had belonged. Therefore, I picked and chose what I would believe to be truth. Although the cult had influenced some of my thinking, it was not the final authority in my thought process.

Later, I discovered people, such as my mother, became my final authority in what I considered to be truth or trustworthy. As I evaluated my standard of truth, I realized I went on the basis of what sounded correct to me. Much of my idea of truth was based on how I was conditioned by those who influenced my life the most.

When I started the spiritual journey to discover truth, I had no idea how deep such influences ran in my life. Granted, the cult may have not greatly influenced my way of thinking, but I still

146

possessed a cult mentality because I did not possess truth. I had my own perverted idea of religious truth that made my way of thinking seem wise, elite, and special.

This perverted way of thinking served as blinders, which kept me from seeing its hypocrisy. I had to realize that what I understood to be truth was wrong. I even had to stay away from the idea that there were some things that could be salvaged in my belief system.

Although, I did not understand it at the time, even the right conclusions had been tainted by a wrong spirit and erroneous indoctrination. Therefore, I had to consider it all as dung and start anew from the right foundation in order to establish a correct belief system. In fact, it was not until 15 years after my conversion that the hidden effects of the cult were completely uprooted out of my life.

The second claim I had to make is that my family was wrong. In our initial innocence, we look to family to establish truth for us. We assume that they know what is true. As they write their form of truth on our clean slates, it takes on an identity of its own. In fact, what we believe becomes a part of our identity. When our beliefs are challenged, it becomes a matter of family pride or honor.

I had to conclude that if the beliefs of my religion were wrong, then my family had to be wrong as well. If my family is wrong, where does that leave me? When a person's foundation is being torn up in such a manner, it must be defended or held on to in order to maintain identity, family unity, and a sense of belonging and purpose.

For most people, separation from family based on truth and religion is frightening and overwhelming. However, the Christian life is found outside the camp of family and religion. Sadly, few ever make the separation or cut that allows them to discover their life in God outside the family or religious camps of what has been considered "normalcy" according to their particular influences.

The final claim I had to make is that I was wrong. We each have to take responsibility for what we choose to believe and how we choose to hear such matters *(Luke 8:18)*. I was told that my cult was right, but I discovered it was wrong. I assumed my family knew what was right, but I found out they were wrong. Obviously, I was misinformed and deceived. My foundation was definitely wrong, and I was wrong for not testing it. I was also wrong to assume those around me knew what they were talking about. I was wrong, and to be made right I had to take accountability for what I believed. I not only had a responsibility to know the truth for myself, but I had a responsibility to line up to it in faith and obedience.

In order to ensure I had a right foundation, I chose the Word of God as my sole authority as to what is true. Although its authority had been undermined by the cult I was involved in, and replaced with man's theology and explanations, I knew that I had to have one standard of truth in which to test all things. Regardless of the attack on the validity of God's Word, I chose by faith to believe it as God's Word, and to believe it as absolute truth in anything concerning God, life, and spiritual matters. Although I did not understand it, I chose to study it to come to an understanding of its truths *(2 Timothy 2:15)*.

When I considered the Word, I did not see how big of a book it was or whether it was boring. I saw it as God's Word that would stand when all else would be considered a lie, a counterfeit, heretical, or worldly. I saw it as a challenge. Its pages contained those things I needed to know to keep me from falling into deception and to live an upright life *(2 Timothy 3:16)*. I did not see reading or studying the Word as a religious duty; rather, I regarded it as the very lifeblood to my well-being. In those initial years of my new life, I readily partook of the Word's pure milk, and in time I developed a hunger for its meat.

At times I would stop and ponder about the possibility that my new life in God was a bad joke. Occasionally, I questioned the logic of putting all of my hope in one book, the Bible. Each time, I was reminded of a very important fact. Since I encountered God as my hope, and His Word as my truth, I had found satisfaction and peace. When I thought about the risk of believing God and His Word, I was reminded of what I told my grandmother the day I debated with her about our differences. The statement I made was, "Grandma, if you are right, I am living a decent life; therefore, I will end up in one of your heavens on the basis of merit. But, Grandma if I am right, you will end up in hell."

As I consider the risk of believing the God of the Bible, and believing His Word as truth, I realize that there was no way I could lose. In fact, to take the other side was to risk everything for something that could not stand, save, or defend a person on judgment day.

Through the different debates over the subject of God, His identity and His Word, I have discovered that faith in the God of the Bible and in His Word is a daily choice. I choose to believe when I do not understand. I choose to believe when logic mocks me for believing God's Word. I choose to believe when circumstances seem more powerful than God. I choose to believe when nothing makes sense to my intellect. I choose to believe because I will not find God in each circumstance without such faith.

Finding God is a daily choice. This means I choose to seek God in each matter and challenge. Through it all, I have found God. In fact, I have found the God described in His Book, the Bible. He has confirmed His identity, authority, and power. He has shown Himself in the small things as well as the big things. In my five decades of being a believer, I have never found God to be a liar, or His Word to be untrue.

Those who come out of a cult with a cult mentality are often like corks bobbing on a sea of confusion, fear, anger, and doubt. The wind of suspicion drives them, the undercurrents of judgmentalism sweep them away from the stability of the Rock, and the waves of uncertainty keep them from ever finding rest, assurance, and healing.

Many cult members struggle with their past, unable to let go of it. Yet, they must let go to seek, discover, and embrace the life God has for them. They keep their past before them to remind them not to trust any religion, rather than learn the lessons of their past so that they can have the liberty to walk in light of the ever abiding present reality of Jesus. They fail to realize the Christian life is never behind them; rather, it is discovered on a daily basis in light of a future, eternal hope.

Are you a former member of a cult? Do you have a cult mentality? I have good news for you. You do not have to continue to be a victim of the cult or a false leader. Jesus came to bind up the wounds of the sheep. However, to bind up your wounds, you must come to Him *(John 7:37-38)*.

You need to give up your right to be a victim, and recognize the authority and power of the Victor. His truth will set you free, His anointing will heal your heart, His authority will subdue the enemy, and His power will enable you to overcome. However, you must come to Him to be healed. You must come to Him to set the record straight about all that was wrong. You must come to Him to transform your perception about Him and life. You must come to Him to exchange your present state of mind with His disposition in order to be reconciled to that which is true and liberating.

As a wounded sheep, a person can claim their right to remain skeptical towards all that is associated with God. As an angry sheep, individuals can maintain their right to determine their own standard of truth. As offended sheep, people can bring accusation against all that reminds them of their religious experience, and feel justified in their rebellion towards God and His Word. As sheep in despair, they can rant and rave about all the injustices they have experienced at the hands of these counterfeits, but in the end all such rights and offences will have to stand before the One who bears the scars that were imposed upon Him by the religious counterfeits of His day. No doubt when such sheep come face-to-face with the reality of these scars, all such rights and offenses will fall silent. Each of these individuals will realize that the goal of every counterfeit of God is to produce counterfeits in His kingdom. It will be at that terrible moment when each person will realize they have become the counterfeit.

On this grave day of reckoning, the everlasting Word of God will ring through the corridors of time and eternity. What will the Word declare in the courts of heaven? Perhaps it will be *Hebrews 2:3, "How shall we escape, if we neglect so great salvation?"*

Or, maybe the words *of Hebrews 6:5-6, "And have tasted the good word of God, and the powers of the world to come, If they shall fall away, to renew them again unto repentance seeing they crucify to themselves the Son of God afresh, and put him to an open shame."*

Maybe the words of Peter will be heard,

> *For if, after they have escaped the pollutions of the world through the knowledge of the Lord and Savior, Jesus Christ, they are again entangled in it, and overcome, the latter end is worse with them than the beginning. For it had been better for them not to have known the way of righteousness than, after they have known it, to turn from the holy commandment delivered unto them. (2 Peter 2:20-21)*

Finally, we cannot forget the words of Jesus found in *Matthew 7:23, "And then will I profess unto them, I never knew you; depart from me, ye that work iniquity."*

The truth is Satan is using cults to win the battle raging for the souls of men. However, we do not have to accept such a defeat in our lives. We can choose life with its blessings, by choosing the real Shepherd of our souls. We can choose the way of faith, freedom, and healing by believing the Word of God. We do not have to accept Satan's way, we can choose to believe, trust, surrender, and put all of our hope in Jesus, and He will raise us above the snare and destructive paths of the counterfeits. As our place of refuge, He will then set us in a large place, a place of rest, victory, and hope *(Psalm 118:5)*.

Prayer

If you can identify with the text of this study and the above testimony, the question is, has the cult come out of you so that you can experience the healing and liberty of Christ Jesus? If not, why not consider the following prayer. Let it be heartfelt as you resolve this issue. Do not remain a victim of a cult, and do not allow it to determine your attitude towards God and the life He offers you. Do not let it undermine the authority of His Word, or strip His truth of its ability to set you free with His eternal perspective. Choose to believe what the Word says, and you will never be ashamed.

Lord,

What can I say? I sincerely searched for You, only to find that which has mocked Your Word, undermined Your authority as God, and made You into a powerless Creator. I am confused. I wanted true religion to only taste of that which was false. I have been wounded, betrayed, and brought to the place of utter despair. I do not know how to believe, and I do not believe I have anything left in me to even reach out to embrace the truth.

However, I have been told that You understand. I have been told that for counterfeits to exist there has to be that which is real. On that basis I choose to believe You are real.

Lord, I have become your lost sheep wandering in a terrible wilderness. I realize that as a lost sheep I am unable to find You. I have also become a prodigal child that needs to finally come home. My only hope is to stand on what You promised according to the parable in Luke 15 that You are the One who will find me.

Lord, hear my cries. I choose to believe You are real, but help me in my unbelief to see You for who You are. I am weary with religion, I am weary with dead-letter doctrine, and I am weary with encountering the same lifeless religious activities. I want what is real, satisfying to the soul, and lasting to the Spirit. I now know I do not want some type of religion; I want You in all of Your glory.

I now come to You in need of mercy, forgive me for settling for the counterfeit. I come to you seeking Your grace, now meet me in your abounding favor to reconcile me back into a living relationship with the one true God. Forgive me for losing sight of Your salvation. Forgive me for neglecting the gift of life, the altar of Your cross, and the benevolence of Your outreached arms.

Forgive me for not loving Your Word, but now I humbly ask that You give me a love for Your truth. Put reins on my walk and bring me under Your liberating yoke. Forgive me for my idolatrous life and ways. I now know Lord, that You are a jealous God and I have exalted idols above You. As a result, I lost sight of You.

Forgive me for the injustices I have shown towards You as God. However, I now know more than ever, I need You. You are the One who will keep my feet on the right path. You are the One who will lead me in the paths of righteousness. You are the One who will heal me in my despair, and lift me out of my hopeless pit. And, it is You alone who deserves my total love and devotion.

As You have promised, give me a new heart that is no longer divided or inclined towards the idolatrous. Give me a new spirit that will be sensitive to Your voice and ways. Cleanse me from all my wicked ways and quicken and renew the joy of my salvation.

I choose to believe by faith that you have heard my cries. I have come to You in repentance, in great need of Your grace, desirous of Your salvation, poor in spirit, and broken by the false ways of my life. I not only choose the life You have for me, but I choose to walk in the ways of Your righteousness. Lord, I commit all to You. I offer up my body to You for Your use and glory. I offer up my mind to be transformed by Your Word and Spirit. I offer up my feeble hands to be used for Your work. I offer my ways to You to be lined up to Your will and purpose. Lord, I offer all to You, and ask You to become my all in all. Lord, just have Your perfect way in my life.

Thank you for hearing my cries, meeting me in my need, answering my heart desire to know You, and honoring me with Your mercy, grace, and forgiveness. Thank You for being the one true, unchangeable God of creation. I now bow before You in humility, knowing You will lift me up, enabling me to see You in Your glory.

I say all this in light of Your name which is above all names, and Your glorious character, ways, truth, and life. Amen.

HE ACTUALLY THOUGHT IT NOT ROBBERY

INTRODUCTION

I have written many books for others, but in this instance, I wrote this book for myself. In essence, it is a long love letter to the Lover of my soul, Jesus Christ. It is a book of appreciation to the One who gave it all. It is a small offering of praise to the One who is beyond description.

This book examines *Philippians 2:5-11,* one of the most powerful revelations of Jesus Christ. I have seen glimpses of this revelation because I constantly refer back to it in my studies, teachings, and sharing the Word.

It is a text that has challenged, matured, and humbled me. Each glimpse has made me appreciate the preciousness of my Lord. Each aspect of the revelation has made me realize how little I comprehend the Lord's love, mercy, grace, and sacrifice.

As I discovered in the text of *Philippians*, Jesus Christ sacrificed far more than His life. These scriptures showed me an ongoing sacrifice being offered, and through this sacrifice I was able to glean what Christianity is truly all about. It allowed me to see the real example Jesus left for each of us who follow Him.

This example is not offered simply to be pondered in our hearts, but must be lived out in every facet of our lives as Jesus lived it when He came to earth. We are told He is the branch from the root of the lineage of David that came out of the barren wasteland of humanity. He became least in disposition, poor in status, marred by the whips of man, and broken by sin as the Lamb of God. The thing I consider most incredible about the ongoing sacrifice of Jesus was His attitude about it: *He actually thought it not robbery.*

There is so much to grasp in these few Scriptures. I feel I will only scratch the surface, but in so doing, I pray that it will bring about godly changes in my life and yours, and bless you as much as it has blessed me.

Enjoy this incredible, humbling journey.

1

THE MIND OF CHRIST

*Let this mind be in you,
which was also in Christ Jesus.
(Philippians 2:5)*

Before we can begin to grasp the incredible principles governing the attitude and life of Christ, we must understand the mind of Christ. First of all, we must ask ourselves, what does it mean to have the mind of Christ? We know the mind is comprised of the intellect, thoughts (or feelings), and the will of a person. How do we come to a place where all three areas openly express the disposition of Christ?

The first insight into what it means to possess the mind of Christ is found in the word *"let."* This word implies you are giving way to something. In this case, you are actually giving way to the person of Jesus Christ.

To give way to something involves the will area. You must make a determination that will begin to govern what you will or will not accept. For example, I recently watched a TV magazine. The interviewers were talking to a homosexual who admitted he did not want to accept his sexual preference. He wanted to be what was considered normal to our society, so he sought out various avenues including exorcism *(note, not deliverance)* to subdue his deviant sexual desires because of his religious upbringing.

After listening to this man, I realized he wanted a quick solution that would immediately allow him to stop thinking and feeling the way he did. He was not willing to acknowledge that it was not an inherited trait, but rather perverted thought patterns that he had personally accepted as reality, and then recognizing them as the darkness of lies that originate with Satan. Such a reality became an acceptable preference to him. This man's unwillingness to take responsibility for his perverted thought patterns kept him from experiencing godly deliverance.

This is how people rationalize and justify perverted lifestyles. False images are erected in the chambers of a person's imagination. Instead of distinguishing a false image as a lie, these confused individuals begin to accept it as their identity and lot in life. Such acceptance will allow them to make peace with their screaming consciences and embattled emotions, supposedly confirming their delusion. No wonder *Proverbs 23:7* states, *"For as he thinketh in his heart, so is he."* It is apparent our identity is determined by what we think on.

This is why Paul exhorted followers of Christ to cast down imaginations that are contrary to the character of our holy God, and bring into captivity every thought to the obedience of Christ. The problem with not casting down imaginations is that you will become vain in your conclusions and bring dishonor to God by giving in to perversion. If you do not take responsibility for your thoughts, you will make a decision to not retain God in your knowledge. As a result, God will give you over to a reprobate mind.[1]

A reprobate mind is where the will gives in to the vanity of the mind. This type of mind is carnal or fleshly and, as the Apostle Paul declared in *Romans 8:6*, such a mind will result in death.

In considering the command to *"Let the mind of Christ be your mind,"* we must acknowledge an exchange has to take place.

---

[1] 2 Corinthians 10:3-5; Romans 1:21 & 28

For instance, I cannot simply choose to put down my carnal mind without having something with which to replace it. I must, therefore, replace my intellect, thoughts, and will with the will, thoughts, and wisdom of Jesus. How do I develop the mind of Christ?

The answer to this question is found in *Colossians 3:1-2*. This passage tells us we must first seek those things that are above. And, how do we seek those things which are above? The answer is simple: Think on them.

Philippians 4:8-9 tells us,

> *Finally brethren, whatsoever things are true, whatsoever things are honest, whatsoever things are just, whatsoever things are pure, whatsoever things are lovely, whatsoever things are of good report; if there be any virtue, and if there be any praise, think on these things. Those things which ye have both learned, and received, and heard, and seen in me, do: and the God of peace shall be with you.*

In *Philippians 4:8* we see a description of Jesus' character. He is true, just, pure, and lovely. He is a person who not only holds a good report in the hearts of those who love Him, but in the very courts of heaven. He is beyond reproach and deserves our praise.[2] Obviously, we are being instructed not only to think on Jesus, but also to seek Him fervently. *Colossians 3:1* confirms this, *"Seek those things which are above, where Christ sitteth on the right hand of God."*

Have you ever done a study on the position of the right hand? For Christ to be on the right hand of God means He is equal and has the same authority or clout. We know He intercedes for us as our High Priest, which makes Him our Mediator. *Psalm 16:11* gives us this beautiful promise, *"Thou wilt shew me the path of*

---

[2] If you would like to know more about Philippians 4:8, see the fourth book the second volume of the Foundation Series entitled, *Think on These Things.*

life: in thy presence is fullness of joy; at thy right hand there are pleasures for evermore." Don't you see? Jesus is the One who represents all our eternal pleasures, and because of being placed in Him, and Him being in us through the presence of the Spirit, we will enjoy such pleasures for ages to come.

The Apostle Paul takes us one step further in *Philippians 4:9*. He tells us we must put into practice what we have learned, received, and heard. Knowledge without application is void of wisdom. This type of ungodly knowledge operates out of pride that is always in competition with God. Obviously, the result is not being able to retain the knowledge of God.[3] Therefore, Paul is instructing us to put our knowledge into practice in order to ensure that God will remain a reality to us.

The kind of relationship we have with our Lord will determine how open we are to receive from Him. When most of us think about receiving from God, we think in terms of blessings and promises. It is true we receive such gifts from God, but we must also be willing to receive instruction and correction, which are also part of the godly package as well.

A good example of a person who could not properly receive from the Lord is Judas Iscariot. This man sat at the same table as Jesus and fellowshipped with him. He witnessed miracles and partook of untold blessings from the hand of the Father because of Jesus. Yet, the man was ungrateful and ended up betraying the long-awaited Messiah. Why? Because he could not properly receive from Jesus, and as a result he abused his privileges and betrayed the Son of God.

When we receive something from God, we have no rights to it. We must seek His face to know how we are to disperse it among others as Jesus did the few loaves and fish among the 5,000.[4] The things of God have the potential to bless others, ultimately bringing glory to Him.

---

[3] Romans 1:28
[4] John 6:1-14

Finally, we must respond in obedience when we hear God's instruction, or else we will find ourselves in opposition to Him. *James 1:22-24* puts it best,

> *But be ye doers of the word, and not hearers only, deceiving your own selves. For if any be a hearer of the word, and not a doer, he is like unto a man beholding his natural face in a glass: For he beholdeth himself, and goeth his way, and straightway forgetteth what manner of man he was.*

The biggest reason Christians fail to develop the attitude of Jesus is because they are not obedient to God's Word. The Scriptures in James tell us if we do not obey the Word of God, we forget what sort of person we really are. We lose perspective and reality. In essence, we are refusing to bring our mind into submission to the Word of God with the intent of obeying it.

It is the Word of God that serves as our mirror and brings a reality check to our spiritual condition. In the life of Christ, we see He was totally obedient to the Father. His intellect, thoughts, and will were the visible expression of the mind of His Father. If He had not been obedient, we would still be miserably dead in our sins with no real hope or future.

It is amazing how much Christians want the best for their spiritual life, but are not willing to be obedient to what has been established as righteousness. If you are not obedient to God's Word, you will never experience His peace until you come into line with His will.

Remember that *Colossians 3:2* instructs us to, *"Set our affection on things above, not on things on the earth."* Here Paul is telling us to set or determine to put our affections or feelings on things above. Again, we see that we must make a determination not to give in to fleshly affections, but choose instead to direct all of our emotions and feeling towards Jesus Christ.

You will find that if you set your feelings on Jesus, a transformation will take place in your mind. Transform means, "to change" or "transfigure." It actually involves a change in form, character, and condition. To transfigure something essentially involves reshaping or fashioning something, which will ultimately manifest a new outward appearance.

The Apostle Paul makes this statement in *Romans 12:2, "And be not conformed to this world: but be ye transformed by the renewing of your mind, that you may prove what is that good, and acceptable, and perfect will of God."* Here Paul is instructing us not to be like, or fashion ourselves according to the world. By giving way to the world, our minds will be molded according to the thought patterns of the world.

Paul also goes on to say, "Be transformed." In other words, bring your mind under the control of God so it will not only be fashioned according to the person of Jesus, but it will become the very expression of His attitude and character.

How are our minds transformed? Paul tells us the change occurs when our minds are actually renewed. Our minds must be renovated, revived, or restored. The only person who can revive our minds is the Holy Spirit. To allow the mind of Christ to be developed in us means we are simply giving way to the work of the Holy Spirit.

In studying *Philippians 2:1-4*, you will see that Paul actually shows us how this mind will function in our relationship with Jesus and others. You can find this description in verse two, *"Fulfil ye my joy, that ye be likeminded, having the same love, being of one accord, of one mind."*

To be likeminded implies you have a similar spirit or motivation. To have the mind of Christ means we will be in agreement with Him since we belong to Him. We are also to serve as an extension of Him in ministry, and that this has been made possible because we have the same Spirit motivating us.

It is this type of oneness that brings joy to the heart of Jesus, and glory to the Father.

Jesus experienced this oneness with His Father, and His prayer request was simple in regards to His followers. Heeding His words in the correct spirit is vital:

> *That they all may be one; as thou, Father, are in me, and I in thee, that they also may be one in us: that the world may believe that thou hast sent me. And the glory which thou gavest me I have given them; that they may be one, even as we are one: I in them, and thou in me, that they may be made perfect in one; and that the world may know that thou hast sent me, and hast loved them, as thou hast loved me (John 17:21-23).*

Notice how this oneness will give visible credibility to the real identity of Jesus in this dark, lost, and dying world. The oneness that Jesus is talking about here is not a product of people coming together for moral or religious good. Rather, this oneness is the result of people coming together because they truly love one Person, and that person is Jesus Christ, and they possess a like-spirit, the Holy Spirit.

If you are giving way to the Holy Ghost, the love of God will come forth in both attitude and action. You will be in love with Jesus, and your life will tell it. As the Apostle Paul said in *Romans 5:5, "And hope maketh not ashamed; because the love of God is shed abroad in our hearts by the Holy Ghost which is given unto us."*

Do you have the mind of Christ, or are your thought patterns a visible expression of the world? To have the mind of Christ is not an option, but a necessity if Christians are going to reach their potential in the kingdom of God.

It is necessary to get to the bottom line on this subject. If you do not have the mind of Christ, you will not be able to follow in His footsteps, which are clearly outlined in *Philippians 2.* Neither will you be able to experience the full abundance of the Christian life.

2

JESUS IN HIS
ORIGINAL FORM

Who, being in the form of God...
(Philippians 2:6a)

"Form" in this scripture means the base or nature of something.[1]
To change form implies the idea of adjusting parts or reshaping
the nature of something. In this Scripture verse we are given
Jesus' identity. It tells us that He was in the form of God. In other
words, He is God by nature.

Today there are many cults and New Age beliefs that deny
Jesus is God by nature. And yet, the Word is very clear about
Jesus' identity. For example, the Apostle John introduces Jesus
as God in the first verse of his Gospel, *"In the beginning was the
Word, and the Word was with God, and the Word was God."* We
know that this verse is in reference to Jesus Christ as the Apostle
John reveals His identity as the Light, Creator, and the Lamb of
God in this incredible chapter.

The Apostle Paul gives us this information about Jesus, *"For
by him were all things created, that are in heaven, and that are
in earth, visible and invisible, whether they be thrones, or
dominions, or principalities, or powers: all things were created by
him, and for him: And he is before all things, and by him all things
consist" (Colossians 1:16-17).* In these Scriptures Paul identifies

---

[1] Strong's Exhaustive Concordance of the Bible; # 3444

Jesus as our Creator, while *Genesis 1:1* identifies our Creator as God.

In *1 Timothy 3:16*, Paul clearly identifies Jesus as God in the flesh, *"And without controversy great is the mystery of godliness: <u>God</u> <u>was</u> <u>manifest</u> <u>in</u> <u>the</u> <u>flesh</u>, justified in the Spirit, seen of angels, preached unto the Gentiles, believed on in the world, received up into glory."* (Emphasis added.) The apostle stipulated that the great mystery of God is that He would come in the flesh.

The Apostle John declared that only those of the antichrist spirit would deny that Jesus Christ came in the flesh.[2] The reality of Jesus being God Incarnate would be verified by the Holy Spirit, witnessed by the angels, preached as a message of hope unto the Gentiles, believed as truth in the world, and confirmed by Jesus' ascension after His resurrection.

Although the Word is quite clear about the deity of Jesus, many choose to explain it away with human logic, erroneous philosophies of man, and doctrines of demons. Believing the true identity of Jesus comes down to faith. We either choose to agree with the Word of God by faith in its declarations concerning Jesus or we reject it by reinterpreting it through other religious lenses and walk in unbelief towards God and His record.

The problem with denying that Jesus is God by nature is that a person will never begin to realize the price Jesus paid for our salvation. By downplaying His divine nature, such an individual will ultimately reject His salvation. God's Word constantly verifies and affirms what it cost the Father and Son to obtain salvation for each of us.

The reality of God's presence, work, and purpose in our lives actually guarantees us of our salvation. It is because of God's character that we can trust Him to save us. The Word tells us Jesus is the only way to salvation.[3] In a sense, He is the ladder

---

[2] 1 John 4:1-3; 2 John 7
[3] Psalm 27:1; Isaiah 12:2; Acts 4:10-12

that connects sinful, insignificant man to his holy God in a living relationship.

We see a type or representation of this ladder in *Genesis 28.* On his way to his uncle's place, Jacob stopped at Bethel for the night.[4] The meaning behind the name "Bethel" set the tone for Jacob's encounter with God. It means "the house of God." At Bethel, Jacob had a dream. He saw a ladder set upon the earth, and the top of it reached to heaven, and the Lord stood at the top of it. He also noted that the angels of God were ascending and descending upon it.

This is a type of Jesus, who became the ladder that came from heaven to earth. Upon Him alone ascend all of our hopes and prayers, and through Him descend wondrous promises and everlasting life. God Incarnate, how glorious is our Ladder! We will be learning for ages to come how the love of God designed a glorious ladder that required Jesus to descend to earth, which would allow man to ascend by His grace and reach heaven.

It was during this dream that the LORD introduced Himself to Jacob. He said in *Genesis 28:13, "I am the LORD God of Abraham, thy father."* When Jesus walked this earth 2,000 years ago, He was forever introducing Himself as the "I AM."[5] His introduction served as a prelude to heart-stirring invitations and judgments.

> *"I am the bread of life: he that cometh to me shall never hunger; and he that believeth on me shall never thirst." "...I am from above...if ye believe not that I am he, ye shall die in your sins." "I am the good shepherd: the good shepherd giveth his life for the sheep." "Verily, Verily, I say unto you, before Abraham was, I am" (John 6:35; 8:23-24, 58; 10:14).*

Oh, what a stir Jesus caused! He brought leadership to the lost, rest to the downtrodden, hope to the outcast, and anger to

---

[4] Bethel was known as Luz before Jacob changed its name to Bethel.
[5] Genesis 28:13

the self-righteous. Men either wanted to worship Him or stone Him. They either wanted to embrace Him as their Messiah or discredit Him by associating Him with the kingdom of darkness.

For Jacob, his encounter with God brought fear. He sensed His holiness and felt that his meeting with God was a dreadful event instead of a blessing. His response should be a warning to us. He recognized God, and it brought a healthy fear to his soul. To face God without intervention is a frightful experience.

The truth is that we will face God in one of two ways. We will face Him within the protection of His grace, or we will encounter His righteousness, judgment, and wrath. How we encounter God on Judgment Day will depend on what we do with His Ladder.

Many different Christs are being presented today, but there is only one God Incarnate. We must recognize the real Jesus for who He is if we expect to come out on the side of God's grace. We must acknowledge that only God could truly provide the acceptable ladder; in fact, He provided Himself, as we will see in the following scriptures in *Philippians 2*.

We see in *Genesis 28:17* that Jacob considered this place a gate to heaven. Jesus said this in *John 10:9, "I am the door: by me if any man enter in, he shall be saved, and shall go in and out, and find pasture."* Jacob may have encountered what He considered to be the gate to heaven at Bethel, but as Christians, we have encountered the true gate or door to heaven in Jesus Christ. The question is how are we to respond to Jesus?

Jacob gives us a beautiful example of what we must do with Jesus. He took the stone his head had been resting upon, erected it, and poured oil upon it. We know according to Scripture that Jesus is the cornerstone that was erected by God, and anointed by the Holy Spirit, but initially rejected by the builders.[6] This is in reference to a popular legend that was well known by

---

[6] See 1 Peter 2:6-8.

the Jewish people surrounding the construction of the temple of Solomon.

All the stones were shaped and cut to the same size except for one. The builders looked at the unusual stone and concluded that it was useless. They cast it into Kidron Valley, which served as their garbage dump. When they were close to being finished, they noticed they lacked one stone: the cornerstone. As they examined the area, they realized the odd stone they had deemed useless was actually the cornerstone.[7]

Apparently, the cornerstone was designed separately from the rest of the stones. According to the information we have about cornerstones, all other stones or bricks were design to be aligned to the cornerstone. Before the temple could be completed, the builders had to retrieve the cornerstone from the garbage dump.

It was obvious that Jesus Christ had come from a different realm. According to Scripture, there is no beginning to Him for He is the Alpha and Omega and the Ancient of Days. The Jewish people initially rejected the cornerstone to their spiritual lives. As a result, He became identified with the worst plight and depravity of mankind on the cross, only to be resurrected in power and glory.[8]

Just as Jacob erected the stone or pillar, the resurrected life of Jesus must be erected in the life of man, who is to serve as the temple of the Holy Spirit. It is when the life of Jesus is being developed within the temple of man's life that the anointing will begin to flow freely to others.[9]

Jesus is indeed the cornerstone of man's spiritual life. He was designed before the foundation of the world to make the life of man whole and complete. He stands out because He is God.

---

[7] Lectures On the Book of Acts by H. A. Ironside, 18th Printing, August 1982, pgs. 105-106

[8] Revelation 1:8; Daniel 7: 9, 10, 13; 1 Corinthians 15:1-4

[9] 1 Corinthians 3:16

This is a thought-provoking statement: If Jesus is not God, we are miserably lost. If He is not God, God's plan would never be carried out on behalf of the world. You might say, "How do you know this?" Because of what happened in *Revelation 5*.

We read that there was a book that needed to be opened in heaven. The angel cried out with a loud voice, *"Who is worthy to open the book and to loose the seals thereof?"* Verse *three* tells us there was not a man in heaven, nor in earth, neither under the earth, who was able to open the book.

The writer of *Revelation*, the Apostle John, claimed he wept much because there was no one worthy to open and read the book. He was finally told by one of the elders to not weep, for the Lion of the tribe of Judah, the Root of David has prevailed to open the book. When John looked to see who the Lion of the tribe of Judah was, he saw a Lamb as it had been slain.

We all know Jesus Christ is the Lion of the tribe of Judah, the Root of David, and the Lamb of God who takes away the sin of the world. But what we must note is that Jesus is no mere man or He would not be able to open the book. Man is wicked and wretched at best, which makes him unacceptable. However, Jesus is the God/Man, and because He is righteous and without sin, He will be found worthy to open the book.

Likewise, Jesus is the light of the glorious Gospel that is able to penetrate the darkness of man's soul. He is the great I AM and worthy of all worship. He is the Lamb of God who became the ultimate sacrifice for our sin.[10] He is Jesus Christ, God Incarnate.

Do you believe this by faith, or are you rejecting God's provision for your salvation by rejecting the deity of Jesus? As John said in his first epistle,

> *Hereby know ye the Spirit of God: Every spirit that confesseth that Jesus Christ is come in the flesh is of*

---

[10] John 1:4-14, 29; 2 Corinthians 4:3-6

God. And every spirit that confesseth not that Jesus Christ is come in the flesh is not of God: and this is that spirit of antichrist, whereof ye have heard that it should come; and even now already is in the world (1 John 4:2-3).

3

THE IMAGE OF GOD

...thought it not robbery to be equal with God.
(Philippians 2:6b)

In the second part of *Philippians 2:6* we see a reference to what we call "the Godhead." We must observe here that even though Jesus was God, He did not think it was robbery when He ceased to be equal with God.

The belief of the Godhead is very controversial. After much study, I have summarized this tenet of faith in the following statement: That within the essence and oneness of the Godhead are three persons: the Father, the Son, and the Holy Spirit. These three persons are co-eternal and co-equal. They are distinct in subsistence, but have the same characteristics or substance. Therefore, the nature of deity of the one true God is manifested in three distinct persons.

People try to understand the Godhead in their own logic. They cannot see mathematically how three persons equal one God. Yet, the Godhead is not a matter of mathematics, but of chemistry. It does not have to do with quantity of something, but with the nature or character of something.

For example, in chemistry we know that two molecules of hydrogen and one of oxygen equal the substance water. Water may manifest itself in different forms such as ice, liquid, or fog, but when you examine the base or nature of any of these substances, you will find it is still water by nature.

This is how the Godhead works. The whole sum of the glory of God has been made apparent through the Father, the Son, and the Holy Spirit. They may come in different forms and have different responsibilities, but they still have the same base nature or characteristics. Therefore, whether you are considering Jesus, regarding the Father, or giving way to the work of the Holy Spirit, you will encounter the characteristics of deity in each person. This is why *Romans 1:20* tells us that creation itself verifies the Godhead, and that in the end man will have no excuse for rejecting this established truth.

It is important that when you consider the Godhead you keep in mind it is actually the nature or characteristics of God that identify Him as being the one true God. Paul's reminder to the Galatians about their spiritual state before they encountered the real God confirms this *in Galatians 4:8, "Howbeit then, when ye knew not God, ye did service unto them which by **nature** are no gods."* (Emphasis added.) Paul is basically telling the Galatians that they were worshipping gods that were not the true God by nature.

We can also find plurality in relationship to the Godhead in scriptures such as *Genesis 1:26; 3:22, 11:7,* and *Isaiah 6:8.* According to Ruth Specter Lascelle, Jewish teacher and author, some of the names of God, such as Elohim, Adonai, and El Shaddai, denote plurality as well. These names are consistently used throughout the Bible. For example, Elohim is used 2,500 times, Adonai 90 times; and El Shaddai 48 times.[1]

We also see reference to plurality in *Philippians 2:6* as well. Jesus thought it not robbery to be equal with God. Let's just consider this one statement for a moment. If Jesus made up the total sum of the Godhead, how could He cease to be equal to

---

[1] Jewish Faith and the New Covenant, pages 62 and 63.

Himself? It is obvious there is more to God than Jesus Christ. In essence this scripture shows us Jesus ceased to be equal to the other two persons of the Godhead.

Keep in mind these three persons of the Godhead were enfolded into the all-encompassing glory of deity through complete agreement. These three persons think, move, and act in total agreement in regard to authority, power, and purpose. However, Jesus stepped outside of this order to take on the disposition of a servant in the fashion or shape of a man. In His humanity, He would have a different relationship with the other two Persons of the Godhead. He would become a son to the Father, and a man who needed to be anointed and led by the power of the Spirit. These two relationships would serve as our examples in light to our lives before God.

The truth about the Godhead is not meant to be comprehended by man's mere mind, but to be received as truth by childlike faith. The problem with the idea of the Godhead is not found in the concept itself, but in man's futile attempt to comprehend an infinite God according to his pathetic logic and limited ability to understand something beyond his present dimension.

Man's logic is limited and perverted at best. When it comes to the things of God, the best man's logic can do is make the person a bona fide skeptic towards all of God's simple truths.

Today there are a lot of skeptics in religion. They have erected God into an image that is acceptable to their logic and requires no childlike faith. The end result to such foolishness is that man possesses an idol constructed by his own imagination or devices. *Acts 17:29* clearly states, *"Forasmuch then as we are the offspring of God, we ought not to think that the Godhead is like unto gold or silver, or stone graven by art and man's devices."*

Colossians 2:9 tells us this about Jesus Christ, *"For in him dwelleth all the fulness of the Godhead bodily."* Keep in mind the term "Godhead" points to deity. In the Person of Jesus is the fullness of deity. Jesus was the complete picture or the visible image or representative of the invisible God in bodily form.[2]

Jesus confirmed this very fact when Philip asked Him to show him the Father. Jesus responded with this statement, *"Have I been so long with you, and yet hast thou not known me, Philip? He that hath seen me hath seen the Father; and how sayest thou then, Shew us the Father" (John 14:9).*

Jesus was the living, visible expression of God. When Jesus spoke two thousand years ago, man was actually hearing the voice of God. When Jesus touched people, they were feeling the hand of God. When Jesus' eye penetrated the hearts and souls of people, they were actually seeing the heart of God reach out to them.

Another term or title that indicated that Jesus was the visible expression of God is that of the "Son of God." Many cults believe Jesus is the "Son of God," but they do not really understand this term, and end up demeaning the very character of Christ. Many erroneously think that God the Father had something physically to do with Jesus' existence by believing He actually fathered Him. In other words, they believe Jesus did not pre-exist before Bethlehem. According to *Vine's Expository Dictionary of Biblical Words*, the term "Son of God" implies that Jesus is the actual, visible expression of God's character and not His biological offspring.

The Jews clearly understood the term "son." When Jesus referred to the Heavenly Father as His Father, He was stating that He was equal with the Father in nature, status, and authority. To the Jews this was blasphemy because it implied that Jesus was God by nature. As you study Scripture, you will see that Jesus' reference to being the Son of God is what justified the Jewish leaders in their pursuit to crucify Him.[3]

---

[2] See Colossians 1:15
[3] Luke 23:67-71; John 5:16-18

Jesus had three other titles that give us a clear picture of Him as the Son of God. He was the Messiah, God Incarnate, and the Savior of the world. We see that these titles show Jesus' position in relationship to the Godhead as the Messiah, His nature as divine, and His purpose as Savior.[4] In order to understand how Jesus was in fact the Son of God, you have to view Him in light of these other three positions. By combining His position, nature, and purpose, you have the revelation of Jesus as the Son of God.

For example, as the Messiah, the Son of man, He served as the reflection of God's power and anointing in His human form. As deity, He was the visible expression of God's attributes, and as Savior He was the reflection of God's heart of love towards mankind. What an awesome revelation! Within the life of Jesus, the fullness of God's love, character, and power was visibly revealed to mankind.

Today is much like two thousand years ago. Many people miss the reality that God walked among mankind. Even though the world would never be the same after His physical appearance, both then and now, few have truly allowed Him to change their lives.

Like today, some groups of people were threatened by Jesus because He exposed the hypocrisy of their creeds and hearts. Others were insulted because He revealed their complacency and false foundations. In some situations, He actually frightened those who did not want their world challenged with the unexplainable.

It is incredible to think God stood among men, and yet men could not see Him because of their arrogance, prejudices, and fear. How many of us do not see Him today? Oh, we may know He exists, but do we see Him for who He is? Do we know Him for who He is? Or, have we allowed Him to walk by without

---

[4] 1 John 2:21-23; 4:1-3, 14-15

changing our lives and situations as He did those of His hometown of Nazareth?

Finally, the Scripture tells us He thought it was not robbery to cease to be equal with God. In other words, something was going to change that would cause Him to cease from being like the other two persons of the Godhead.

Hebrews 2:7 gives us this insight, *"Thou madest him a little lower than the angels."* Now think about this for a moment. Jesus, who is God, did not feel He was being robbed when He was made lower than those He created.[5] If you or I were in a similar situation, we would be crying foul. We would probably throw a big pity party and walk around telling everyone how we were being treated unfairly.

However, in the case of Jesus we see a different attitude and response. He never considered it unfair that He was not equal to God for the first time in His eternal existence. He did not throw a pity party when He was made lower than those who worshipped Him in the courts of heaven. Instead, He willingly embraced it all, giving the impression it was an honor to be demoted in such a way.

Are you beginning to get a small glimpse into the disposition of Jesus? It is obvious that Jesus was not watching out for Himself. It is clear that He had no personal agenda or something to prove. The truth is He did it for you and me. He did not do it because we deserve His intervention. He did it because of God's incredible love towards man. And, when godly love is the motivation, no sacrifice is too great. In fact, it will be a person's good pleasure or honor to offer any required sacrifice.

Love is the secret behind why Jesus counted it as a privilege to come by way of Bethlehem as a babe in a manger and leave by way of a rugged cross as the ultimate sacrifice. This is why the Apostle Paul gave this instruction in *Philippians 2:3, "Let*

---

[5] Colossians 1:15-18

nothing be done through strife or vainglory; but in lowliness of mind let each esteem others better than themselves." After all, Jesus left us with such a powerful example.

How about you? Are you living in agreement with or in compliance to the example given you? If you are not, it is obvious that you have neither the love of God nor the mind of Christ.

4

HE EMPTIED HIMSELF

But made himself of no reputation...
(Philippians 2:7a)

In our self-serving, self-centered humanity and society, it is hard to imagine what it meant for Christ to empty Himself. First of all, how did He empty Himself? Secondly, what did He empty Himself of?

I believe the answers to these two questions will only be fully revealed in eternity. I also sense as we gain even a slight revelation into this one small section of Scripture, we will be humbled and overwhelmed by the implications of what it is saying.

The initial truth we must recognize up front is that Jesus is the one who made Himself of no reputation. This means to empty oneself of something. In other words, it was His sovereign choice to give up something.

I remember reading the book *In The Footsteps of Jesus* by Bruce Marchiano. Bruce was the one who played Jesus in the Matthew Video Series. One of the incidents that brought a reality check to me surrounded the crucifixion. Mr. Marchiano and the director were ready to make Jesus appear to be an innocent, suffering, mistreated victim. Just before they were about to do the scene, the director approached Bruce and said the Lord had actually told him, "Don't be sorry for Me." Sadly, the suffering, week martyr is how Jesus has been presented in much of the media, especially in the movie, *"The Passion."*

It is important for each of us to realize that Jesus was in control of His destiny. He made the choice to walk the route to Calvary. Man did not take his life; rather He offered it up as an offering from God on our behalf.

When Jesus went to the cross, He did not go as a victim but as a willing sacrifice. After all, a victim has no rights to choose, but Jesus always had a choice. He could have turned back at any time, but He chose to become the glorious, victorious Lamb of God who would take away our sin.[1] Praise God for His choice and His sacrifice.

In a way, this is true for us. Our choices determine our eternal destiny. Every day we either choose Christ and heaven or we give way to Satan and hell. In order to choose heaven, we must be willing to empty ourselves daily of that which would keep us from realizing our potential in the kingdom of heaven.

On the other hand, the path to hell is broad. A person would only have to make one decision to find himself in the clutches of this tormenting place. This decision is often borne out of the sin of omission where faith and righteousness are omitted in a matter. And, what replaces righteousness towards the character and ways of God?

Complacency is how we justify or qualify our lukewarm attitude and actions towards God. Indifference of this nature results in a person making a decision to reject God's truth, provision, and way in attitude and lifestyle. Since many, out of complacency, give way to the natural man, hell has enlarged its borders to embrace them.[2]

In this Scripture we see Jesus initially made a decision in heaven that would allow Him to pay the necessary price on earth for our salvation. This decision was not a matter of good

---

[1] John 1:29; 10:18
[2] Isaiah 5:14

intentions. In fact, this Scripture implies this decision was of such magnitude that it could not have been spontaneous on His part. We also see in Jesus' physical life on earth that this determination was reinforced on a continual basis until it was fully carried out. *Luke 9:51* states, *"He stedfastly set his face to go to Jerusalem."*

This is a very important lesson for Christians and those who put off salvation. People often postpone making a total decision to love and follow Jesus until they have experienced the attractions of the world. They see themselves as making the right decision when the time comes. Such a conclusion is a false security.

The truth is that preparation must take place that will enable a person to stand in uncertain times. Such preparation begins with small steps of obedience that lead to greater feats inspired by abiding faith in God in the midst of great trials.

Another lesson we see from this scripture is that Jesus' decision to empty Himself came from His attitude. In essence, Jesus actually gave way to something that would not benefit Him personally because of His excellent disposition. He surrendered to something contrary to His very person so we could benefit.

People who are self-centered in their attitude will never come to a place where they will yield to anything unless it serves their purpose. They will never consider accepting less unless they get some heroic recognition for it.

This is where we begin to see how contrary the real attitude of Christ is to the self-centered disposition of man. In light of Jesus' disposition, we see how man's pride is exposed for its insidious ways, and his flesh for its unscrupulous practices. We begin to see how hypocritical the heart of man can be because it is quick to accept delusion, while verbally claiming to love a person by the name of Jesus.

The next question is how did He empty Himself? As we will see in the next scripture, He made an exchange in order to accomplish such a feat. According to my *Webster's New Collegiate Dictionary*, "exchange" is the act of giving or taking one thing in return for another. Jesus gave up His glory in relationship to His sovereignty as God to take on the disposition of a servant and the form of a man.

The word "glory" means honor, beauty, and majesty.[3] Jesus, as God, gave up that which distinguishes Him the most as God. He gave up the majesty that would bring Him due honor and praise, as well as the heavenly beauty that would set Him apart from mankind. Jesus did not give up His nature as God, for He could never cease to be who He is. Rather, He gave up His capacity to be God. "Capacity" points to His power and authority as God. As already pointed out, He gave up His sovereignty as He ceased to reign as God in His majesty, and became subject as a servant to the authority of others.

As I studied this, I had to ask myself, "Why did Jesus have to give up this aspect of His glory as God?" As I meditated on this provoking thought, the Holy Ghost was gracious enough to remind me of what happened when God appeared to man in His glory. When God met with Moses in the burning bush in *Exodus 3* and Joshua in *Joshua 5*, they were both told to take off their shoes because they were standing on holy ground.

In *Exodus 20*, we see God speaking to the people of Israel. His majesty was evident as people heard the thundering and noise of the trumpet and saw the lightning and smoke surrounding the mountain. Instead of savoring the moment, the people became afraid and asked Moses to serve as their intercessor between them and God. Now keep in mind that the people of Israel were told that if they touched the mountain they would die. After all, it was holy ground.

We see a total contrast in what happened centuries later. People encountered God in the form of Jesus Christ, but they did

---

[3] Strong's Exhaustive Concordance of the Bible, #1391

not have to take off their shoes. They heard His voice, but they did not become frightened, and they touched Him but did not die. When you consider these events, you begin to gain some insight as to why Jesus as God had to take on humanity not only to become the Lamb of God but to cloak the fullness of His glory so He could walk among man.

In two separate incidents, mere man actually witnessed or encountered the implication of Jesus' glory as God. We see the same responses coming from the witnesses as we do from those in the Old Testament who encountered God in His majesty. The first situation occurred on Mount of Transfiguration. Jesus' humanity gave way to His glory as God for a few minutes. The Word of God tells us Jesus' face did shine as the sun and his raiment was white as the light. In the midst of the transfiguration, the voice of the Father was heard. *Matthew 17:6* tells us the voice caused the three witnesses, Peter, John, and James, to fall on their faces in fear.

The second incident happened in *Revelation 1*. The Apostle John had a revelation of Jesus' unhindered glory that caused him to fall at Jesus' feet as if he were dead. In other words, it took his breath from him, and he almost fainted from fear. Consider this for a moment. The Apostle John was one of those who were on the Mount of Transfiguration and witnessed His glory. He was also the one who laid his head on Jesus' chest the night He was betrayed. Jesus had entrusted His mother to John, and yet when John saw Jesus in His unhindered majesty, he practically fainted from fear.

Jesus gave up His glory and became poor for us. The Apostle Paul confirms this in *2 Corinthians 8:9, "For ye know the grace of our Lord Jesus Christ, that, though he was rich, yet for your sakes he became poor, that ye through his poverty might be rich."*

It is because of God's grace that Jesus became poor so we could become rich. Being rich does not mean rich according to the world, but rich according to what we can have spiritually in Christ. Today some doctrines teach that if you are a Christian, you should be rich in material goods. According to the Apostle Paul in *1 Timothy 6:3-12,* this is a blatant error we must flee from.

Oswald Chambers stated in *Daily Thoughts for Disciples,* that people have become afraid of being poor, and despise anyone who is willing to be poor in order to save their life. He goes on to explain that this spiritual poverty means liberation from material attachments, an unbribed soul, indifference, and being able to find value in who we are in Christ, and not what we do or have in this present world. This liberty means we have the right to fling away our life at any moment in an irresponsible fashion.[4]

Jesus made an incredible exchange that meant He acted contrary to His very person. He gave way to something that would not benefit Him. He gave up His glory to take on that which would cause Him to be lower than the angels. He did all of this so we could be spiritually rich.

What does it mean to be spiritually rich? Perhaps James summarizes the real measure of the riches that the citizen of heaven should ultimately value and pursue in this present world in *James 2:5. "Hearken, my beloved brethren, Hath not God chosen the poor of this world to be rich in faith and heirs of the kingdom which he hath promised to them that love him?"*

Faith is established in us as we follow Jesus. For example, by faith we must follow Jesus' example. He emptied Himself of His glory; therefore, we must empty ourselves of all of our vainglory, or, in other words, our pride. After we empty ourselves, we will be able to make the ultimate exchange.

Let us now consider what Jesus actually exchanged for His glory. By understanding it, we will get a glimpse of how much God loved us. We will also begin to sense in a small way just

---

[4] May 21st devotion.

how far He went to reach us in our depravity in order to save us unto eternal glory.

5

THE POSITION

...and took upon him the form of a servant.
(Philippians 2:7b)

To me *Philippians 2:6-11* is one of the most powerful summaries of Jesus' journey to Calvary. It gives us a small glimpse as to the price He paid, allowing us to see the choices He made in light of our eternal destination. We also can observe the steps He took that started in eternity and ended on an old rugged cross.

In the last chapter I talked about the fact that Jesus made an exchange. He gave up His glory in order to give way to something else. According to *Philippians 2:7*, we see Jesus gave up His glory in order to take on the form of a servant. In summation, He adjusted His very essence by miraculously taking on the disposition of a servant.

What an incredible revelation! Jesus, who is God, became least so you and I could taste the greatness of eternity. Jesus, who deserves service, became a servant so we could become children of the Most High God.

It is important that we realize that Jesus made a decision to accept this lowly position in the courts of heaven long before He executed it on earth in an earthly body. He actually agreed to come into total subjection as a servant in every area of His humanity.[1]

---

[1] 1 Corinthians 2:7; Revelation 13:8

Keep in mind the position of servitude is considered the highest place in the kingdom of God, but among mankind it is considered the lowest rank. Jesus made this contrast clear to His disciples in *Matthew 20:25-27:*

> *Ye know that the princes of the Gentiles exercise dominion over them, and they that are great exercise authority upon them. But it shall not be so among you: but whosoever will be great among you, let him be your minister; and whosoever will be chief among you, let him be your servant.*

Charles Spurgeon referred to Jesus as the Servant of servants. This is an awesome insight into the very heart of the example Jesus left for us to follow in spirit and truth. In order for Jesus to be considered a Servant of servants, He actually became a servant to mankind.

The truth is all people are born into servitude, but do not necessarily possess the disposition of a servant. In reality everyone is serving something. They either serve sin, self, or the world, which brings them under the dominion of Satan, or they serve the living God of all creation.

Jesus, who is God, submitted Himself to a position of great servitude. This position was designated in heaven and carried out in the earthly tabernacle of a body. Once again, we must realize that Jesus made a choice to take on such a position. He actually made a decision to give up His rights as God to sovereignly reign over His creation. This meant that He gave up His strength and power as God to call the shots. Ultimately, He became a living sacrifice for the glory of the Father and to benefit those He came to serve.

Jesus simply gave up that which was normal to Him. He gave up the glories of His heavenly residence. He gave up comfort and conveniences of the sanctuary of His heavenly kingdom. He also gave up His place in the courts of heaven. He gave up His authority and came under the authority of another.

We see this giving manifested in Jesus' humanity as well. As King of kings He had rights to a palace and prestige that would have required even the earthly leaders to pay homage to Him. Instead, we see that He gave up His rights as king in order to live the life of a servant. Jesus confirmed this with these words, *"Foxes have holes, and birds of the air have nests; but the Son of man hath nowhere to lay his head" (Luke 9:58).*

Jesus' decision and choice are so contrary to the attitude of man. It is hard for arrogant, self-sufficient man to come into submission to something that would never benefit his self-serving agenda. It is hard for stiff-necked humanity to give way to something that would require giving up the comforts and conveniences of life. In fact, it is beyond narrow-minded humans to comprehend how the idea of greatness is measured by becoming the least when they actually strive to become God of their personal domain.

Jesus gave up the normal (heavenly) and took on the contrary (servitude). His actions contradicted the teaching and preference of man. Man may pursue the contrary, but all the time he clings to normalcy. After all, the idea of giving up the normal (rights to self and the world) in order to embrace the contrary (the righteousness of God) is mockery to unregenerate man.

Let me bring the previous thought into focus. It was contrary for Jesus as God to take on the limitations of a servant. It is also contrary for fallen, depraved man to take on God's righteousness. The fact that Jesus stepped through such boundaries to reach you and me so we could be made the righteousness of God shows His power and commitment as God to do the impossible.[2]

Through the years the Lord has allowed me to experience the normal life promoted in America, but I have learned to hold lightly to such comforts and conveniences for they are temporary and

---

[2] 2 Corinthians 5:21

belong to Him. If He requires any convenience from me, I must be quick to relinquish it in order to give way to the eternal.

It is amazing to observe how, when Jesus started giving His all in order to obtain our salvation, He never stopped even after He offered Himself as the ultimate sacrifice. He is still in heaven serving as our Priest and point of defense as our Advocate. Oh, how can any of us neglect such a salvation?[3]

Realizing that godly servitude carries a certain attitude with it is also important. Without the right attitude, a servant of God will fall short of service that will glorify God. We see this godly attitude in Christ. He actually described His disposition in *Matthew 11:28-30, "Come unto me, all ye that labor and are heavy laden and I will give you rest. Take my yoke upon you, and learn of me: for I am meek and lowly in heart: and ye shall find rest unto your souls. For my yoke is easy and my burden is light."* Out of a right disposition, Jesus expressed Himself in an attitude of meekness. The word "meek" implies power or strength under control.

We see the reality of Jesus' attitude of servitude when He walked this earth. As a servant, He gave way to the will, instructions, and authority of the Father. Jesus said this in *John 5:30, "I can of mine own self do nothing: as I hear, I judge: and my judgment is just; because I seek not mine own will, but the will of the Father which hath sent me."*

We see from this Scripture that Jesus was totally under the authority of the Father. We must also note the Father was the One who sent Him. In other words, Jesus in his humanity did nothing unless the Father ordained it. Keep in mind Jesus was still God, but His strength and power were now in total subjection to the will of the Father.

How many of us would submit all of our power and strength to someone else? How many of us would only respond in

---

[3] Hebrews 2:3; 7:24-26; 1 John 2:1

controlled strength when given permission to do so, even when faced with suffering and death?

My friend, this is what godly meekness looks like. It only operates within the confines of righteous servitude. It never takes liberty outside of the Master's will, or claims personal rights when circumstances are unfair. It simply means the will, mind, and emotions have come into total subjection to the Master.

Psalm 37:11 and *Matthew 5:5* tell us, *"The meek shall inherit the earth."* I used to meditate on this concept. How can the meek overcome or conquer the earth enough to inherit it? As I considered Jesus' life, I realized that because of His meekness neither was He swayed nor did He become subject to circumstances or earthly persecution that always seemed to follow Him. As a result, He overcame all the claims the world had on His humanity, and conquered Satan and the circumstances that surrounded Him.

This is a very important principle for Christians to understand. It is vital that we bring every area of our lives under the leading of the Holy Spirit. If our strengths are not disciplined properly, we will find ourselves being tossed to and fro by the waves of circumstances and change.[4] Instead of overcoming the world, we will be subdued by it. Instead of conquering our circumstances, we will end up being controlled by them.

Jesus was also lowly. "Lowly" means cast down, humble, and of low degree or estate.[5] Jesus declared that He was lowly in heart. His disposition was felt in every fiber of His being, which produced humility. This low estate allowed Him to prefer you and me to His own well-being. As a result, He gave way to the earthly so we could experience the heavenly.

This attitude is upheld throughout the New Testament. An example of this attitude is found in *Romans 12:10, "Be kindly*

---

[4] Ephesians 4:13-14
[5] Strong's Exhaustive Concordance of the Bible, #5011

affectioned one to another with brotherly love; in honour preferring one another."

Ephesians 5:21 states, *"Submitting yourselves one to another in the fear of God."* Godly submission means you are honoring or putting other people's needs above your own. You are actually giving way to that which is worthy or excellent to ensure the best results in a matter.

This preference is evidence of godly humility. Many people try to fake this humility, as did the Pharisees in Jesus' time. The piousness of these people was simply outward, but it lacked true love. It was often self-centered; therefore, it fell short of being sacrificial. It displayed itself in religious actions, but was never obedient to the will of God.

Jesus left a precious example. A real servant is an obedient servant. Jesus was obedient in every way to the Father. You and I must be obedient as well to qualify as true servants of God. In fact, we have been given a book of instructions that establishes how we must conduct ourselves in every area of our lives, from attitude to sacrifice.

Let me ask you something: Are you a servant of God? Jesus showed us true servitude in action, and He led the way in example. Are you following in His footsteps?

6

THE IDENTITY OF
THE MAN, JESUS

...and was made in the likeness of man.
(Philippians 2:7c)

Have you ever thought about how our infinite God combined His eternal state with an earthly, finite state? He actually allowed Himself to be made in the likeness of man while maintaining His eternal attributes of God.

I already discussed what it meant for Jesus to be God, and how He emptied Himself of His sovereignty to take on the form of a servant. However, we need to realize the form of His servitude was visibly expressed in His manhood.

Something else that is important for us to recognize is that Jesus was not made or shaped in the likeness of just any man. He was molded into the likeness of a perfect man. He was an example of the first Adam before he gave way to rebellion in the Garden of Eden.

Scripture confirms the fact Jesus was the second Adam or the second man in 1 *Corinthians 15:45*. *"And so it is written the first man Adam was made a living soul; the last Adam was made a quickening spirit."* In considering Jesus, we can actually begin to see man's potential, which was lost in the Garden of Eden.

Oswald Chambers put it best in his teaching found in *Bringing Sons Into Glory* as he explained how Jesus as the second man manifested what the human race is going to be. He is the God-man, the representative of the whole human race in one person. He is not a being with two personalities, but rather He is the Son of God who is the exact expression of Almighty God, and the Son of Man who serves as the presentation of God's normal man. As the Son of God, He reveals what God is like, and as the Son of Man, He serves as a mirror to what the human race will be like at the basis of redemption. This picture points to a perfect oneness between God and man.[1]

In *John 16:7-11*, we are told that the Holy Spirit has come to reprove the world of sin, righteousness, and judgment. We see how the Holy Spirit uses the inward conscience of the Law to convict man of sin, but He uses the example of Jesus Christ to reprove the world of unrighteousness. Jesus is the example of what the acceptable, perfect man looks like from within. If we do not have a right heart and attitude, we will fail miserably before God regardless of how righteous we may appear outwardly.

Failure to allow the Holy Spirit to convict us of sin and reprove us of unrighteousness brings us under judgment along with the god of this world. This is why the Holy Spirit always leads us to Christ, who is our mirror regarding our true spiritual condition before God.

1 Corinthians 15:47-49 tells us,

> *The first man is of the earth, earthy: the second man is the Lord from heaven. As is the earthy, such are they also that are earthy: and as is the heavenly, such are they also that are heavenly. And as we have borne the image of the earthy, we shall also bear the image of the heavenly."*

In short, Jesus touched pathetic, earth-bound humanity with the heavenly reality of God.

---

[1] Bringing Sons Into Glory & Making All Things New; ©1990 by Oswald Chambers Publication Associations Limited. page 16

Jesus gave up the heavenly to take on the earthly. Likewise, we must give up the earthly to take on the heavenly. He brought the reality of perfect man to our attention. He is calling us to take on the image of this heavenly Man in spirit and truth. The heavenly Man possesses that which is pure and upright. This Man who has been quickened from above will live forever.[2]

Oswald Chambers put this concept in perspective in *Bringing Sons Into Glory* by pointing out that Jesus came from the outside into the human race, and once a person is born again, the very life of Jesus comes into them from the outside. He is a normal man, and in His relationship to God, the devil, sin, and man, we can see the expression in human nature of what Jesus calls "eternal life."[3]

Jesus, the Son of God humbled Himself and became the Son of Man to not only reflect a heavenly man, but a normal man. Jesus came to relate to man in a way that would not only give him a reality check, but also a way to reach his heavenly potential and embrace eternal life.

The title "Son of Man," which Jesus used of Himself throughout the Gospels, holds great significance. According to *Vine's Expository Dictionary of Biblical Words*, the title "Son of Man" is a messianic title. This is brought out when Jesus is referred to as the "Son of David." The title associates Him with both man and the promised Messiah. And, as you study Isaiah's prophesy of the Messiah in *Isaiah 9:6*, the Messiah is also identified as "The Mighty God."

All of man's hopes and God's promises hinged on the coming of the Messiah, Jesus Christ. He was anointed to heal the brokenhearted, set the captive free, and give sight to the blind, and liberty to those who have been bruised by the harsh realities of life and sin.[4]

---

[2] John 3:3 & 5; Romans 8:29
[3] Page 15
[4] Luke 4:18-19

As man, Jesus was the example of true leadership in the kingdom of God. According to *Vine's Expository,* the title of "Son of Man" went beyond the messianic title to universal headship on the part of One who is man. For example, Jesus is the head of a universal body, the Church. The four creatures found throughout Scripture, the lion, ox, man, and eagle, symbolize His universal leadership.[5]

As the Lion of the tribe of Judah, He became the Lamb of God. As the Lamb, He showed the real strength that comes from authority and power in godly leadership. Such leadership is always expressed in gentleness and meekness. Jesus, as the ox, shows that enduring strength and leadership that comes through the discipline of the yoke and sacrifice that is motivated by godly love.

As the Son of Man, He showed how man must become the crowning glory of God through example. It is important to point out that headship implies leadership by example, not by harsh demands and dictates. Jesus left us with two distinct examples as man. The first example is found in *John 13*, which we have already discussed in the previous chapter. A man must become a servant of all if he is to become great in leadership in God's kingdom.

The second example Jesus left us as man is found in *1 Peter 2:21-22, "For even hereunto were ye called: because Christ also suffered for us, leaving us an example, that ye should follow his steps: Who did no sin, neither was guile found in his mouth."* Jesus was without sin, and yet He suffered, leaving us an example.

There are a couple of reasons we must encounter suffering. The first reason we must taste the bitter dregs of suffering is because it works character in us. The Apostle Paul made reference to this in *2 Corinthians 4:17, "For our light affliction,*

---

[5] Ezekiel 1:10; Revelation 4:7

which is but for a moment, worketh for us a far more exceeding and eternal weight of glory."

One of the conditions that will bring suffering to our lives is godliness. The Apostle Paul confirms this in *2 Timothy 3:12,* *"Yea, and all that will live godly in Christ Jesus shall suffer persecution."*

The Apostle Peter takes a person one step further in *1 Peter 2:20, "For what glory is it, if, when ye be buffeted for your faults, ye shall take it patiently? But if, when ye do well, and suffer for it, ye take it patiently, this is acceptable with God."*

Godly suffering allows you to become identified with Jesus. This identification will bring glory to God, allowing man to be God's crowning glory in the midst of great despair and darkness. The Apostle Paul put it this way, *"But we all, with open face beholding as in a glass the glory of the Lord, are changed into the same image from glory to glory, even as by the Spirit of the Lord...if so be that we suffer with him, that we may be also glorified together."* [6]

As the eagle, Jesus shows us that godly leadership can only be done in light of a heavenly perspective. Jesus soared above the world because He did the Father's will. He overcame the world because He considered all things in light of eternity. And, because of His type of leadership, He will rule the world as the King of kings.

The Word also tells us that the man Jesus is sitting on the right hand of God. As previously stated, there is much meaning and symbolism in relationship to the right hand, mainly that of authority. We also know scripturally that all pleasures are at the right hand of God. *Psalm 16:11* makes this declaration, *"Thou wilt shew me the path of life: in thy presence is fulness of joy; at thy right hand there are pleasures for evermore."* We know that Jesus is on the right hand of God; therefore, all of our hopes and

---

[6] Romans 8:17c; 2 Corinthians 3:18

promises can only be found in Jesus. No wonder the Apostle Paul told us to seek those things above, and to set our affections on that which is in heaven.[7]

Jesus did not give up His manhood after His death on the cross. It is incredible to believe, but Jesus is still totally man. He is in a different body, but He is still man.[8] It has taken me years to realize the significance of Jesus keeping His manhood. I know my understanding of it is still very limited, but it has proven to be humbling and life-changing to me. Jesus needed to keep His manhood to fulfill vital positions and functions in heaven. These positions actually ensure our very salvation.

The foremost position He fills as a man in heaven is that of High Priest. *Hebrews 5:1* tells us that the High Priest must be taken from man and *8:1* states, *"Now of the things which we have spoken this is the sum: We have such a high priest, who is set on the right hand of the throne of the Majesty in the heavens."*

Jesus established an unchangeable priesthood in heaven. As *Hebrews 7:25* tells us, *"Wherefore he is able also to save them to the uttermost that come unto God by him, seeing he <u>ever</u> <u>liveth</u> to make intercession for them."* (Emphasis added.) Think about it. As the Son of Man, Jesus is able to make the intercession for each of us that maintains our salvation. This intercession makes Him our Mediator.

The Apostle Paul made this statement in *1 Timothy 2:5, "For there is one God, and one mediator between God and men, the man Christ Jesus."* Once again, we must note there is only one mediator. He is identified as the man, Christ Jesus.

Jesus does not stand in the gap for us as God, but as man. Meditate on this incredible insight: Jesus has the power to shed His manhood and return back to His original state, but somehow the maintenance of our salvation hinges on His manhood. Once again, we must acknowledge our salvation is so very important

---

[7] Hebrews 8:1; Colossians 3:1-3
[8] John 20:15-17

to the heart of God. I know we will be spending eternity learning the significance of Jesus as man sitting in the courts of heaven as our High Priest, interceding on our behalf.

Over the years I have caught glimpses of the importance of Jesus' being man in the judgment halls of heaven. We know that to be a good intercessor, you must understand the position of the one you are interceding *for*, as well as understand the mind and heart of the one you are interceding *to*.

Jesus clearly understands both positions. *Hebrews 4:15* tells us He was tempted in every way, but yet He did not sin. Jesus' experiences as man allowed Him insight into the struggles of humanity. His insight as man not only gives Him a personal understanding, but also gives Him the authority to stand in the gap for each of us. This is why John refers to Jesus as our advocate in *1 John 2:1*. He stands in the courts of heaven and becomes our point of defense when we fall into sin and disgrace.

Romans 11:33-34 tells us, *"O the depth of the riches both of the wisdom and knowledge of God! How unsearchable are his judgments, and his ways past finding out! For who hath known the mind of the Lord? Or, who hath been his counselor?"* No mere man could stand in the place of an advocate for mankind, but Jesus could because He took our place on the cross. He also possesses the wisdom and knowledge of God. He is righteous; therefore, He knows the judgments of God, and has satisfied them as our Advocate. He knows the complete mind and heart of God; therefore, He is able to uphold the righteousness of God, while standing in the gap for us.

Sometimes I have envisioned Jesus serving as my advocate in the courts of heaven. Because He is positioned on the right hand of God, I know He actually has the ear of the Father. In my heart I do not see Him fervently standing up defending me with the skill of a great orator for in sin I stand guilty. I do not see Him pleading for mercy for my wretched soul. Rather, I see Him simply standing and lifting His arms up as silence falls in the judgment hall.

You might be wondering why I could believe such simple actions on Jesus' part could silence the accusers or spectators in heaven. Years ago I realized that heaven was perfect in every way except for a few discrepancies. And, what are those areas of blemish? They are the nail-pierced hands and feet of Jesus. I believe all Jesus has to do to intercede on our behalf is stand up and reveal those nail scars.

These scars remind all of heaven that Jesus paid for our sins, and that redemption was completed on the cross. It verifies that through Jesus' scars He became sin on the cross, and upon our salvation we were made perfect in Him because of His wounds. After all, it was His blood that once ran from those scarred places that cleanses us from all unrighteousness. This very same blood represents a new covenant that brings everlasting life and provides a way into intimate fellowship with God.[9]

As you try to logic out the possibility of Jesus being totally God and totally man in heaven as He was on earth, it becomes too great to comprehend. In His humanity, He could not cease to be God. Apparently, in His glory, He cannot cease to be man. However, in my studies I have concluded that if Jesus had stripped away His manhood, He would have given up His greatest point of mediation on my behalf. As I meditated on this humbling fact, I wondered how I could so easily forget what He has done for me.

I am aware that every time I take communion, I am remembering what Jesus did on the cross. I ask myself, "Do I remember with humility and intensity? Do I remember that Jesus still sits in heaven with the evidence of my own wretchedness, bearing precious scars that will be with Him for eternity?"

---

[9] Zechariah 13:6; John 14:6; 2 Corinthians 5:21; 1 John 1:7; Hebrews 10:10-20

How humbling it is to think the one perfect man will remain "physically blemished" to ensure our salvation! It is also sobering to realize His blemishes will overshadow every bit of our imperfection. It is incredible to think how many people shun what Jesus did for them, and heartbreaking to see how many people neglect His salvation.

Let me end this chapter with a challenge. Oswald Chambers has left us with insight about perfection in *Bringing Sons Into Glory*. He stated that we try to enter into Jesus' life by imitation instead of His life entering into us by means of His death.[10] Obviously, this is a wrong approach. His people clearly need to reflect Him and not try to play or imitate Him in a world of skepticism and darkness.

---

[10] Page 15

7

THE HUMILITY OF CHRIST

And being found in fashion as
a man he humbled himself.
(Philippians 2:8a)

Have you ever thought about the humility of Christ? This part of the Scripture tells us that being found in fashion as a man He humbled Himself. As man, Jesus encountered all the limitations of the flesh. He felt hunger and thirst. He knew what it meant to be tired. He felt joy as He embraced a child, and rejoiced as He gave back the dead to the grieving. He felt sorrow over lost mankind and the pain of man's cruelty. He felt both the tearing of His skin and heart. He knew what disgrace felt like as He heard the scorn and mockery of man. He tasted both betrayal and His own blood.

In studying Jesus' life, we see the constant display of Christ's humility. His example should serve as a reality check that will expose our pride in its many forms. His humility goes beyond an outward show of piety to reveal a commitment that reached beyond eternity to grasp the insignificant. For example, the Son of God humbled Himself and embraced the insignificant when He came into this world as a vulnerable child.

In fact, Jesus' allowing Himself to go through the natural process of birth is both miraculous and overwhelming to the finite mind. Jesus allowed Himself to be fashioned as a man. He had given up His capacity as God to take on the form of man. Although His mother was of this earth, He was not from this world. Therefore, He did not inherit the selfish disposition of Adam. He had the disposition of a servant, subjected to His Heavenly Father, and without sin.[1]

Jesus' birth actually caused travail for Mary, His mother. Of course, this travail would pale in comparison to the travail He would experience on a cross to bring eternal life to man.

As an unborn child, He easily could have been aborted if His unwed mother had been stoned according to the Jewish Law because of her untimely pregnancy. From all religious appearances His conception was sinful, not miraculous as the angels had proclaimed. In spite of all the obstacles, Jesus would live for the main purpose of redeeming man from sin's awful consequences so each of us would not have to pay the full penalty of it. His death on the cross appeared as if religion was justified for its rejection of Him, but His resurrection would prove differently.

As a newborn baby, His very presence became a threat to the leader, Herod. This wicked man pursued the child in order to destroy the existence of not just any future leader, but the existence of the ultimate leader.

There are many "Herods" in today's world. They are forever blinded by their desire to be the supreme ruler of their small worlds. They are jealous when it comes to the idea of relinquishing their world to someone who is worthy and greater.

In Herod's blind jealousy, he ended up doing the unspeakable. He sacrificed all the male children in Bethlehem, from newborn to two years old. What a great atrocity! So many innocent children died because of one man's blind obsession. However, Jesus, the Lamb of God, was preserved so that He could become the ultimate sacrifice for all men. [2]

---

[1] John 3:31; 8:23; Hebrews 4:15
[2] Matthew 2:16-18; John 1:29

It is humbling to grasp the humility of Christ in just this area of His life on earth. The idea that Jesus came into this world in a natural way as a helpless babe, totally dependent on those around Him, is indescribable. However, His wonderful humility goes beyond the indescribable.

Keep in mind that Jesus came into this world through the door of a manger. Here was God, the Lord of lords, King of kings, surrounded by the residues and odor of animals. In a way, it was symbolic of how one day He would take upon Himself the filth and dirt of all mankind. He would wear the depravity of humanity with great compassion and sorrow. His grace and love were always being extended, but humanity would often remain indifferent to His invitations.

We see how Jesus' humility was visibly represented by the fact that He was always surrounded by the insignificant. His mother was a poor handmaiden, and his adopted father, a carpenter. He was born in an unimportant place called Bethlehem, and He grew up in Nazareth, a place that was often overlooked and ridiculed.

According to *Smith's Bible Dictionary*, people from Nazareth were considered with contempt. Apparently, the Nazarenes spoke with a ruder dialect and were considered less cultivated. They were greatly exposed to heathen influence because Nazareth was located near the well-traveled highway between Egypt and Mesopotamia.

Nazareth, in spite of its location near a popular highway, had a certain measure of seclusion. According to *Reader's Digest's Great People of the Bible and How They Lived*, Nazareth's population was only around 100 residents in Jesus' time. It was also located halfway between the ocean and the Sea of Galilee.

It was in this place that Jesus submitted Himself to obscurity. The Son of God grew up without any type of notoriety. He lived a quiet life and was known only by those in His small community. This community simply assumed that Jesus was just another member of its small group. The residents had no idea that they were witnessing God in human form. He walked among them and had favor among them, but few would realize that one day they would bow their knees before Him and proclaim Him to be Lord.[3]

As I meditated on Jesus' development into manhood, I could see how Nazareth was an ideal place for His growth. He must have seen, in the passing caravans, people of different nationalities. He witnessed their diversities as well as their similarities. In essence, He witnessed and encountered the activities of the world without becoming part of it.

In the immediate terrain of Nazareth, Jesus was surrounded by ruggedness, which was symbolic of the profession that He was trained in. It is amazing to think how God Incarnate, the Creator of the world, was trained to be a carpenter.

I have no doubt Jesus was an exceptional carpenter. He was a man who could effectively work with His hands. He probably fixed broken plows and cart wheels, mended equipment, and built furniture. I wonder if He ever thought about the day His hands would be used to touch humanity in a way that would forever change its course. He would actually heal broken hearts, mend hopeless lives, and begin to build an eternal kingdom that would abound in the hearts of men.

In this obscurity Jesus was being prepared for a greater feat. As a carpenter, He most likely developed muscles as He wrestled with the wood to conform it to a design or purpose. This rugged profession would prepare Him to endure one of the greatest physical challenges as He found His body being conformed to a wooden cross.

He probably learned how much stress He could put on the wood before it was rendered useless. This may have served as an example to Him as He experienced all the temptations of

---

[3] Luke 2:51-52; 4:22

mankind. He must have realized there were limitations, and that lasting endurance could only be found within the framework of faith and righteousness.

Like Nazareth, which was halfway between the ocean and the Sea of Galilee, Jesus had to be aware that He stood between God's greatness and man's limitations. Because of His position He would be able to accomplish the impossible. He would actually bridge the gap between the powerful and what appeared to be the insignificant. This connection would bring forth rivers of Living Water that would revive the souls of man and bring eternal life to the hopeless and dying.[4]

It is also humbling to consider the one example Jesus left us during this period of obscurity. He was 12 at the time. I am sure you know the story, which is found in *Luke* chapter *two*. Jesus had traveled with His parents to Jerusalem for the Passover. After the celebration, His parents assumed He was with other family members. They were a day into their journey before they realized Jesus was not among them. He was actually missing.

Imagine how these parents must have felt. A missing child for any length of time brings great dread to the hearts of any responsible, loving parent. Keep in mind Jesus was not just any young boy. God had entrusted Him to Mary and Joseph. It was as though through assumption and neglect these parents had mishandled or misplaced something precious from God.

I know in my Christian life I have mishandled the things of God. I have assumed much about God's will and man's soul. I have neglected the gifts of God because I took for granted the spiritual life that comes by way of God's grace.

This incident also made me wonder if I would notice if Jesus' presence was missing in my life. It is so easy to get caught up with the moments of celebration and life that we quickly leave Jesus behind. It is not unusual to become lost in the bustle of the

---

[4] John 7:37-39

world so that we are not aware that something precious and vital is absent.

The discovery of Jesus' absence caused His parents to go back to Jerusalem, the place where they had left Him. On the third day they found Him in the temple, sitting in the midst of the doctors, both hearing and asking questions. This timing would serve as a prelude to Him being in the grave for three days, hidden from all, only to be rediscovered alive after His triumphant resurrection.

Luke 2:47 tells us, *"And all that heard him were astonished at his understanding and answers."* In this Scripture, we see Jesus' wisdom and maturity being evident at a young age. However, it is important to point out that in the Jewish culture a boy steps into manhood at the age of 12. Here we get the first glimpse of Jesus as man. He is among the religious, challenging them with answers that astonish those around Him.

His mother asked Him how He could cause such worry for them. Jesus' answer in *Luke 2:49* is simple but profound, *"How is it that ye sought me? Wist ye not that I must be about my Father's business?"*

As a young man, Jesus is not only aware of His spiritual responsibility and purpose, but He is committed to it all the way. He may have been considered a young man who was exceptional in every way, but He was also obedient to the higher moral law of His Father. This moral law required Him to come into subjection to His parents. Once again, we see God Incarnate submitting Himself to the insignificant in *Luke 2:51, "And* (Jesus) *went down with (His parents), and came to Nazareth and was subject unto them."* (Parenthesis added.)

I am sure most of us are aware of the fact that many of our children begin to declare their independence during their initial teenage years. When we compare Jesus' reaction, we begin to see how His example should silence all rebellion and cause each of us to adhere to the higher moral law of God.

Recognizing authority in our life is a necessity because it establishes us in righteousness. When you think about it, Jesus could have removed Himself from under His earthly parents' authority with the noble goal to submit to the ultimate authority. After all, He is God and possesses wisdom from above.

The truth is Jesus was submitting to His ultimate authority when He submitted to His earthly parents. Submission to the proper authority is the righteous response of a godly man. It is the evidence of unwavering strength that comes through discipline. Submission, in fact, is the highest form of discipline in the kingdom of God, and is a product of humility that recognizes the importance of that which often seems insignificant. It is often the insignificant points of our lives that develop character and prepare us for future challenges.

I have watched many people fight against coming into godly submission. They consider anything that does not serve their purpose insignificant to the growth and promotion of their lives. They want their way, claiming their independence to seek what they consider a better and more substantial method. What these people do not realize is that godly submission ensures liberty while independence causes bondage and destruction.

As you can see, liberty is not the same as independence. Independence has no real boundaries, but liberty works within boundaries or disciplines that encourage a person to reach their highest potential.

The Apostle Paul talked about this discipline which comes out of submission in *1 Corinthians 9:26-27, "I therefore so run, not as uncertainly; so fight I, not as one that beateth the air: But I keep under my body, and bring it into subjection: lest that by any means, when I have preached to others, I myself should be a castaway."*

Godly submission results in humility. This type of submission is manifested through the will, emotions, and actions. Jesus showed this submission when He came into subjection to His parents.

Jesus, as our example, shows us that no matter how old we are or what kind of relationship we are in, submission is never out of date in the kingdom of God. It is a godly virtue that is exemplary of righteousness. It is a necessary ingredient when it comes to being about our Father's business.

Do you have the humility of Christ that can be seen in submission to what you might consider to be insignificant?

8

"NOT MY WILL"

...and became obedient.
"Philippians 2:8"

Oswald Chambers pointed out that Jesus will remain a mental abstraction that may be spoken of in terms of culture, poetry, or philosophy, but will have no meaning or power over a person until He becomes incarnate.[1] This has been confirmed by my own personal experience with God.

Before Jesus became a reality to me, God seemed far away and foreboding. It was not until I encountered Jesus in His humanity that I began to consider God in a personal light. He had seemed unreachable until the voice of the Son of God penetrated my heart. He seemed unfeeling until I realized the Son of Man cried over pending judgment and destruction. God, in fact, seemed indifferent to my struggles until Jesus became the Great Physician who came to bring healing to my pathetic, lost soul. He had appeared to be insensitive until I witnessed Jesus as the Lamb of God walking up Calvary with the cross. He also seemed deaf to the plight of all mankind until I realized that as the Man of sorrows His heart was actually broken on the cross for each of us.

Jesus in His fullness as man expressed the fullness of God in love, mercy, and grace. He made God, who seemed so far

---

[1] Daily Thoughts for Disciples, August 4

away, personal to finite and helpless people such as me. While on earth, Jesus revealed the power of God in miracles and deliverance, the will of God on His way to Calvary, and the heart of God on the cross.

We can actually observe the reality of God's heart towards man in the culmination and climax of Jesus' manhood on earth in His final days before the cross. We can see the shadow of the cross becoming more distinct as He came closer to it. After all, the cross was His real destiny. It had simply been a subtle shadow cast throughout the Old Testament, but it was about to become a harsh reality that would reveal the extent of God's love towards mankind and the devastation of sin upon mankind in light of our Creator's holiness.[2]

In studying Jesus' final days before His crucifixion, I discovered the path He took. It revealed the ultimate purpose of why He came as man. *Luke 9:51* tells us that Jesus steadfastly set His face to go to Jerusalem. In other words, Jesus' determination to finish His greatest course as man became more set as the time drew closer to embracing the cross.

According to the Gospel of John, Jesus was at a place called Bethany six days before the Passover. Bethany was located 1½ to 2 miles from Jerusalem on the road from Jericho. Its name means "house of dates" or "house of misery." I believe the real countdown to the cross began here.

The timing for Jesus being at this place was significant. This is where He was separated or anointed for His death and burial as the Lamb of God by Mary, the sister of Lazarus. He would become a sacrifice for all sin.[3]

In an article in the February 1999 issue of, "Bible In the News," a valuable rundown of Jesus' last six days before the cross was presented. It caused me to contemplate the countdown to the cross in a way that I have never considered.

---

[2] John 3:15-17
[3] John 12:3-7

This publication pointed out that the anointing probably took place on the fifth day before the cross. As pointed out in the article, this would be significant because lambs designated as the Passover lamb were anointed on a Sabbath, five days before the actual Passover.[4] Since Jesus was the complete fulfillment of the Passover Lamb, He would have been anointed on the fifth day as well.

It is important to realize that in order for Jesus to become the Lamb of God, He had to take on the form of a man. As a perfect, sinless man, He could offer Himself up as the true Lamb of God who had clearly been foreshadowed by all of the previous Passover Lambs.

If the time table is correct and Jesus was anointed as the Lamb of God on the fifth day, He was finally acknowledged as King on the fourth day. Instead of presenting Himself as a victorious King, He rode a colt in humility while people took palm branches and went forth to meet him, crying, *"Hosanna: Blessed is the King of Israel that cometh in the name of the Lord."*[5]

Amazingly, within four days of this event some of the very same people most likely would be yelling, "Crucify Him!" Oh, how fickle we human beings are! How self-centered and self-serving we can prove to be. It is true; at the door of every unbroken and unrepentant man lays incredible treachery against God.[6]

We also see Jesus' tears flow the same day after His triumphant entry into Jerusalem. His status as the greatest of all prophets among mankind had become apparent. His appearance had actually been prophesied in *Deuteronomy 18:15-19.*

This ecstasy and great distress or sorrow can be found in the life of every servant of God. I know, as a minister, I have experienced both in one day.

---

[4] Exodus 12:3, 5
[5] John 12:12-16
[6] Hosea 6:7

As a prophet, Jesus considered the future of Jerusalem. However, His response was not that of a victorious King who was embracing His future residence or kingdom; rather, it was of lament and sorrow as He prophesied its future destruction.[7]

History reveals that Jerusalem is the city that has been sacked most often. According to Ruth Specter Lascelle, Jerusalem has been besieged 47 times and completely brought to the ground 17 times. It is estimated that every 75 years the city of peace has been encompassed by enemy armies, and every 200 years it has been left in ruins.[8]

Right now Jerusalem is at the center of great conflict. Three major religions want to claim this city as their religious capital. Presently, Israel is fighting for its very survival against terrorism. Much of the world is pushing for a Palestinian state to usher in peace. But it will never happen because Jerusalem will be the main obstacle that will prevent all of man's attempts of peace. Ultimately, the city that was ordained and designated by God, will become a cup of trembling to the whole world.[9]

Jesus could see the future plight of His precious city. One day He would come as King and reign from it, but until that time, Jerusalem would be at the mercy of fierce and unrelenting Gentiles. These Gentiles would abuse it and ignore the place it holds in the hearts of the Jewish people, and in their future as a nation.[10]

On the third day, Jesus' prophetic office continued as He exhorted the religious leaders, and for the second time in His ministry chased out the merchants and moneychangers from the temple. The number three has an important significance. It represents "entirety" or "completeness." Keep in mind that at the beginning of Jesus' ministry three years earlier, around the same

[7] Luke 19:41-44
[8] Jewish Faith and The New Covenant, page 34.
[9] Zechariah 12:2-3
[10] Daniel 9:24-27

time, He went into the temple and overturned the moneychangers' tables.[11] He had such contempt for those who abused the ordinances of God and took advantage of the religious lives of the less fortunate.

It is possible this second incident implied Jesus' earthly mission (not heavenly ministry) was about to be completed. I often wonder what Jesus would do in some of our modern-day church buildings. Would He throw over the espresso and hotdog stands or maybe knock down booths in the foyers that advertise the latest golf tournament for a so-called charity? Or, through tears, He might condemn the lust that is prevalent in the Christian realm to have bigger, better church buildings that offer more entertainment and silly programs in order to attract greater numbers of people, while showing absolutely no regard for the needy. What would He do? Would it cause the same opposition? Due to the opposition His actions caused He went back to Bethany.

On the second day before Passover, Jesus expounded on the events surrounding the end days.[12] Here we see Him as the Great Prophet laying out a prophetic picture for the future. The blueprint was quite clear, but the exact timing was left as a mystery.

On the day before the presentation of the Passover Lamb, Jesus celebrated the Feast of the Unleavened Bread with His disciples. It was a solemn time. Jesus informed the group that one of them would betray Him. What is most amazing to me was how many of them asked Him if they were the guilty party. It was as though they had come to realize the potential of treachery that waited at the doors of their hearts.

Jesus would lift up the bread and declare that it represented His broken body. He would hold up the wine and proclaim it represented His blood, which was symbolic of a new covenant.

---

[11] Mark 11:11-15; John 2:14-17
[12] Luke 21, note 21:37-38

He would state that it would be their last wine together, *"...until that day when I drink it new with you in my Father's kingdom."* Isn't it wonderful how Jesus started out with harsh realities, but ended with the promise that one day His followers would feast with Him in the presence of His Father? We now know He was pointing to the wedding supper of the Lamb.[13]

I am sure the disciples had questions about the meaning behind Jesus' declarations. He had told them that He would die, but the reality of it all had eluded them.

Their next stop would be the Garden of Gethsemane. Andrew Murray, in his book, *God's Will: Our Dwelling Place*, made this insightful statement, "Gethsemane! The innermost sanctuary of the life of our Lord and of His great redemption." In some respects, it is even more mysterious than Calvary."[14] Here Jesus would encounter His greatest test as man. In our finite state we are unable to understand the extent of this test, but His Word gives us glimpses that should bring humility and sobriety to our spirits.

In the Garden

It is important to point out that it was in a garden that a man by the name of Adam lost his initial state of innocence. It was in a garden that the gap was established between man and His Creator. It was in a garden that Satan and deception won over truth and righteousness. This first garden was known as "Eden" or "Paradise."

The second garden, Gethsemane, displayed the opposite contrast. It was known for the olive press that would squeeze the precious oil out of the olives. The first garden was beautiful and perfect, but the second garden was void of such majesty. In the first garden, the first man lost paradise because of disobedience,

[13] Matthew 26:28-29; Revelation 19:6-10
[14] Page 46

but in the second garden, the second man reestablished paradise through obedience.

At this time I feel the need to make an important statement. *The battle for souls was lost in the Garden of Eden, but won in the Garden of Gethsemane.* Jesus had to come to a garden as man in order to pass the test that was lost in the Garden of Eden. Here we see the greatest form of obedience. This obedience came out of self-denial that resulted in great suffering. *Hebrews 5:8* confirms this, *"Though he were a Son, yet learned he obedience by the things which he suffered."*

What was the great temptation that brought great suffering to the man Jesus? Was the temptation the cross? Hardly! Jesus came just for the cross. Was it the suffering? No, Jesus reached out to embrace the bitter dregs of man's cruelty and Satan's mockery when He was arrested.

Whatever this great temptation was, He had to contend with fear in His humanity. *Hebrews 5:7* confirms this, *"Who in the days of his flesh, when he had offered up prayers and supplications with strong crying and tears unto him that was able to save him from death, and was heard in that he feared."*

Oswald Chambers believed the great temptation Jesus was facing was not death or suffering, but was the fact that He would be fighting this battle in weak flesh.[15] I tend to agree with him because of what Jesus said to Peter in *Matthew 26:41b,* *"...the spirit indeed is willing, but the flesh is weak."*

I believe the Garden of Gethsemane is where we see the great battle of the flesh. Man had lost the battle of the flesh in the Garden of Eden when he partook of the deadly fruit. However, Jesus had to win this battle in spite of unbearable temptation.

Out of obedience Jesus was ready to drink every bit of the bitter cup, but the test would come along the lines of His humanity, not His deity. It would be on the basis of His humanity

---

[15] Bringing Sons into Glory & Making All Things New; page 123

that He had to pass this test because there would be no second chance. Could He actually make it to the cross after enduring a continual assault on His flesh to become the sin offering, so man could be made in the righteousness of God?[16] He was willing to crawl if need be to die for us, but would His flesh succumb to the unmerciful persecution before the price could be paid in full? His preparation for this time had begun in eternity and He had come so far. Obviously, He could not fail no matter how weak the flesh.

Jesus could not allow the physical afflictions to overcome His flesh before He made it to Calvary. He could not allow the cross to silence His cries before He had fulfilled His purpose.

Jesus had two judgments to face before He faced God's judgment on the cross. He had to stand before a self-righteous Sanhedrin Counsel that was bent on crucifying Him. He would next face the judgment of the Roman Political system at a place called "Gabbatha." The leaders would treat Him as a hot potato, tossing Him between each other as if He was some form of entertainment. He would face their judgment of indifference, as well as a whipping that could cut a man in half.[17]

Obviously, Satan was playing a big part in Jesus' temptation in the Garden. It was Satan's final chance to throw everything at Jesus. No doubt the liar was bombarding Him with doubts as to whether He would endure to the end or fail to finish the course due to His weak flesh.

We cannot begin to imagine the depth of Jesus' trial in Gethsemane. *Hebrews 4:15* tells us He was tempted in all points and yet without sin. In the past I have often viewed His success over temptation in light of His deity. Now I realize He overcame the worst type of temptation as man. He truly became our example.

No matter how weak the flesh, Jesus ultimately knew His destiny was not in the hands of the religious leadership, but in

---

[16] 2 Corinthians 5:21
[17] Matthew 26:57-66; 27:1-2

the hands of His Father. He would make a determination to bring His will in line with the Father as He declared, *"...thy will be done."*[18]

This battle in the Garden became so overwhelming that it brought Jesus to the brink of death. It was so great that an angel came from heaven to minister to Him.[19] He truly became a man of sorrows in the Garden of Gethsemane. He was being crushed like olives are crushed. He was pressed from every side by the incredible weight of the sin of all mankind. In spite of the great struggle, Jesus submitted His flesh under the will of the Father to do with as He pleased as He once again proclaimed, *"...nevertheless not my will, but thine, be done" (Luke 22:42b).*

Jesus ultimately knew that neither the political system nor the religious leaders had any say over Him. They had been placed in authority for such a time as this.[20] They were limited according to God's plan, and it would not be thwarted in any way.

The account in *Matthew 26* shows us that Jesus submitted His will to the Father three times. Keep in mind the world is made up of the lust of the flesh, the pride of life, and lust of the eyes.[21] Each submission showed His willingness to become a sacrificial lamb, ready for the slaughter, as a means to address the influences of sin upon man, as well as face the three judgments that were before Him.

It is vital to point out that the cross represented the victory of the Son of God, but the Garden is symbolic of the victory wrought by the Son of Man. In a way, Jesus offered a sacrifice in the Garden of Gethsemane. He actually offered His humanity as great drops of sweat, as of blood, fell to the ground.[22] It was as if all the rights and dictates of His manhood were being emptied

---

[18] Matthew 26:42
[19] Luke 22:43
[20] John 19:10-11
[21] 1 John 2:15
[22] Luke 22:44

out on the ground. He was giving way to the Father's will in the midst of the greatest type of testing.

Perfection was lost in the Garden of Eden by Adam and regained in the Garden of Gethsemane by Jesus. Man's rebellion won out in Eden, but obedience overcame temptation in Gethsemane. *Hebrews 5:8-9* give this insight, *"Though he were a Son, yet learned he obedience by the things which he suffered. And being made perfect, he became the author of eternal salvation unto all them that obey him."*

Adam lost his innocence in the Garden of Eden, but Jesus as the Son of Man was made perfect because He refused to give in to the dictates and fears of the flesh and the temptation of the god of this world, Satan. Instead, He gave way to the will of the Father.

Jesus had won the initial battle for our souls by submitting all of His humanity to the Father. He overcame the weaknesses of the flesh in order to go to Calvary. These are important examples to keep before us. All battles must first be won in our flesh before we can be victorious on the frontlines. In other words, we must deny self before we will be able to pick up our cross to be in the will of God.

So often Christians desire the anointing and power of God over the approval of God. They want to experience all of His blessings, but the battle must be first won in the gardens of the world: self, heart, mind, and the will of man. In every battle there will be choices. We can give in to temptation and lose paradise, or we can submit all to the will of God and overcome and gain the heavenly.

Jesus had successfully faced the failures of the flesh in light of the judgments wrought by the religions and governments of man. Now He could face the judgment of God for sin on the cross in light of victory.

Since Jesus won the battle of the flesh, He was able to ensure His destiny as the Lamb of God. It was His obedience to the Father's perfect will that established His perfection as man. Such obedience allowed Him to take His next step towards the cross as the perfect, sinless sacrifice.

Believers must realize that they will visit the Garden of Gethsemane throughout their Christian life. They will travel the route of Calvary. They will experience the separation that comes with anointing for God's purpose, and feel the joy of victory as they see Jesus lifted up as King. They will feel the sorrow as they consider the lost souls of men when they bring them warnings of future events that will go unheeded. They will know the sweetness of communion, as well as the bitterness of sacrifices, only to be tested in the Garden of Gethsemane where they will feel the crushing press of temptation.

There are two different responses that occur in Gethsemane. A person's response will determine whether they will succumb to temptation or complete the course. The first example we have is Jesus Christ. If we come to the garden to be in obedience to God's will, we will experience a breaking and crushing that comes from self-denial. In fact, we will become identified with Jesus, and as a result will be glorified with Him.[23]

The second example is Judas Iscariot. In the Garden of Gethsemane, he ended up betraying the Son of God with a kiss. This second response represents those people who just want to play the religious game. They give Jesus lip service but their hearts are far from Him.[24] Flesh is still calling the shots while pride is demanding attention and exaltation. They ultimately will betray Jesus in their lifestyles and actions.

Have you been to the Garden of Gethsemane lately? If you have, what was your response? Did you become identified with Jesus by allowing yourself to be crushed, or did you betray Him with a kiss?

---

[23] Romans 8:17
[24] Matthew 15:7-9

9

"IT IS FINISHED!"

...became obedient unto death,
even the death of the cross.
"Philippians 2:8"

It is erroneous to think that Jesus came into this world to be a martyr. In fact, to imply that Jesus came as a martyr is to demean the reason He came. If He had died as a martyr, He would have been dying out of conviction for a principle. In fact, He would have given His life for something worthy or noble.

Jesus Christ did not die for a principle, but rather He died for each of us. He did not die for us because we were worthy of His sacrifice, but He died because we could not change the direction of our eternal, destructive destination. He did not die out of noble reasons; He died because He could do no less due to who He is, God Incarnate.

Oswald Chambers explained that Jesus' death on the cross was not a matter of martyrdom, but was His job description or vocation.[1] The word "vocation" means a work in which one is called. Jesus was ordained to die for you and me. He knew before the foundation of the world the route He would travel to secure our salvation as our sin bearer.

Some Christians give the impression that Jesus went to the cross out of sympathy because He was so good. *2 Corinthians*

---

[1] Bringing Sons Into Glory & Making All Things New, pgs. 63 & 69

5:21 clearly states He became sin. This shows us that it was not a matter of sympathy or goodness but one of identification. This identification was necessary in order for Jesus to become a substitute sacrifice for each of us on the cross.

Philippians 2:8 also tells us His death was a matter of obedience. Jesus' whole being had one goal: to obey His Father in heaven. Each step of obedience led Him closer to the cross. As a result of His obedience, He was never out of step. He never took a detour or swayed from the course. He had come for one purpose—to die—and not only would it be an act of obedience, but it would bring glory to the Father.

Scripture clearly declares that as Jesus got closer to the cross, His inclination and determination to reach the cross became greater in order to fulfill the destiny that had been laid upon Him as Man.[2] Jesus' death as the Lamb of God was the ultimate act of submission and obedience to the will and heart of the Father.

On the cross, man's depravity was exposed and God's love revealed. On the cross mercy and judgment came together to produce grace. On the cross forgiveness won out, paradise was promised, and love reached out in a personal way in the midst of great sorrow and suffering. It was on the cross that thirst represented man's true spiritual condition and showed how bitterness, not comfort, tries to silence its cries. In fact, on the cross the cause for man's deepest spiritual sorrow, that of separation from God, was unveiled.

On the cross we have the representation of man's worst and God's best. We see the love of God overcoming man's hatred. We see arms reaching out to graciously accept acts of gross rejection from men in order to enfold them into the everlasting arms of love.

---

[2] Luke 9:51

The cross of Christ brought the greatest darkness, only to give way to the light of glorious resurrection power. The cross caused the earth to shake, only to offer peace to all who would receive its work. It stood as the greatest form of humiliation, defeat, and destruction, only to be exalted as a place of salvation and victory.

I have felt overwhelmed thinking about the cross of Christ. There are not enough words to describe how far the cross of Christ has reached into my soul, how much it has affected my life, and how wondrous it has become to me.

I have often meditated on trying to put the cross of Christ into words. I had to ask myself, is there one word that could describe its work? Could any number of words properly portray the hope it offers, or any one statement explain its eternal effects?

Surprisingly, the answer is "yes." The one word that is able to describe the work of the cross is, *"redemption"*. The hope of this rugged instrument can be summarized in three words, *"It is finished!"* The one statement that could explain its eternal affects can be found in *Ephesians 2:16, "And that he might reconcile both unto God in one body by the cross, having slain the enmity thereby...."*

Jesus came to redeem hopeless, lost man. Redemption is a term related to money. It means to buy or repurchase something. Did Jesus actually buy something when He went to the cross? *1 Corinthians 6:20* and *7:23* state that each of us has been bought with a price. He bought back our very souls from the jaws of death.

It is clear Jesus paid a debt we could not pay. In other words, we do not have what it takes to make ourselves acceptable to God or satisfy His Law. Our best is filthy rags, and the most we can give God in our own power is lip service and a prideful self-righteousness that ultimately ends up judging Him in some way.[3]

---

[3] Isaiah 64:6

Hebrews 9:22 tells us what kind of tender was used to pay this debt, *"And almost all things are by the law purged with blood; and without shedding of blood is no remission."* Jesus' blood was the principle payment, while His sufferings and pain could be considered the interest payment.

We have been bought with the blood of Jesus, which serves as a new covenant. This covenant or agreement allows us to enjoy an intimate, personal, childlike relationship with God. It gives us identity, rights to an eternal inheritance, and access to the heart of God. It gives us purpose and direction.

As we can see, Jesus not only went the distance when He went to the cross; He also went the extra mile for us. He not only sacrificed on our behalf, but He became the sacrifice. He not only gave His best; He gave His all. He not only went to the cross; He went to the grave. He was not only resurrected; He ascended to heaven to serve as our High Priest and Intercessor. Jesus not only took the necessary steps to obtain our salvation at Calvary, but He went beyond the cross to heaven to ensure it.[4]

Because Jesus paid the full price for our sins on the cross, the work of redemption was completed. This is why Jesus was able to cry out, "It is finished." In other words, we can do nothing to secure or add to the work of redemption. If we try, we frustrate the grace of God and are giving way to another gospel.

It is Jesus alone who saves. To try to add anything to the work of redemption is to make a mockery out of His death and the price He paid.[5] Redemption became a bridge in the spiritual realm. It connected lost man to His loving Creator. This connection is also known as reconciliation. *2 Corinthians 5:18* gives us this insight into reconciliation, *"And all things are of God, who hath reconciled us to himself by Jesus Christ, and hath given to us the ministry of reconciliation."*

---

[4] Hebrews 7:25
[5] See Galatians 2:16-3:3.

According to *Vine's Expository Dictionary of Biblical Words,* reconciliation is the New Testament term for atonement. The difference between these two words is as obvious as the difference between the Old and New Covenants. Atonement means "covering" while reconciliation goes one step further. It implies that an actual exchange took place.

For example, the blood of animals simply covered a person's sins under the Old Testament, but on the cross Jesus took away our sins by becoming a substitute for us, establishing the New Testament or Covenant. As He became sin (or sin offering), He provided an avenue for us to be made into the righteousness of God. We are no longer just covered; we can now be restored. We no longer have to worry about making other sacrifices because Jesus' sacrifice was sufficient, and we can now walk in liberty before our Lord.[6]

This New Covenant means that the common person, including you and me, can now come boldly to the throne of God without fear and personal effort to commune with Him. We can bring every concern, problem, and desire before the One who desires to be our Father, husband, and constant companion.

This New Covenant also means I can enter into a new agreement with God. This agreement is not based on a corporate Law that could neither justify nor make a person righteous. Rather, it is based on grace that justifies and allows a person to stand righteous before God through faith in what Christ accomplished on the cross.[7]

The new agreement can also be found in the type of relationship Jesus is forming with His Body, the Church. It is a marriage relationship.[8] This type of relationship points to one of the most powerful bonds that can exist between two parties. It is a relationship that implies agreement in all three areas of man,

---

[6] Hebrews 9:12-24; 10:10-22; 1 John 1:7 & 9
[7] Ephesians 2:8-10
[8] Ephesians 5:21-33; Revelation 19:7-9

the spirit (heart), soul (mind), and body. If the bond is upright, it is unbeatable in quality and unbreakable in strength.

Finally, this new agreement of reconciliation ends in peace. This peace is for real and can only be found when a person has finally made peace with God through Jesus Christ. *Matthew 5:9* says it best, *"Blessed are the peacemakers: for they shall be called the children of God."* We can only be peacemakers because we have spiritual well-being. We can only have spiritual well-being when we have finally entered into the pure relationship as children of the heavenly family, dependent heirs of God.

Reconciliation lies at the heart of the ministry of Christ. Granted, His ministry was motivated by His incredible love. Mercy and grace inspired Him to reach beyond the depths of man's unlimited depravity and despair to bring much-needed hope. Obedience guided each step, commitment each action and compassion allowed Him to rejoice, cry, and die on a cross. But the truth is that His heart was to reconcile man back to the one true God.[9] This reconciliation results in salvation and restoration.

What Christ accomplished on the cross is miraculous and incredible. This old rugged altar stands as an eternal line that has caused many to stumble in their attempts to avoid or reject its message. It appears to be a foolish fable to those who want to continue to be contrary to God. It has caused much debate, confusion, anger, and sorrow. It requires a decision of agreement or rejection. In the end, it will either save or judge.

There is no doubt that this cruel object stands between life and death. It looms between defeat and victory, and stands tall in the shadows of light and darkness. It serves as a curtain between truth and deception. Even now, more than 20 centuries later, it casts an indisputable shadow over those who reject it,

---

[9] 2 Corinthians 5:18-19; John 14:6

and shines as a star of hope to those who are seeking life, truth, and hope.

The cross of Christ lies at the core of the greatest story ever told and the revelation of the greatest life that was ever lived. It will remain in the journals of eternity as the ladder that reached heaven, the bridge that closed the great gap between God and man, and an ugly instrument that revealed the glory, power, and love of God in light of sacrifice, suffering, and death.

The question you must ask yourself is what have I done with the cross of Christ? Does it represent a fable or absolute truth? Does it represent foreboding, vanity, sorrow, or great joy? Does it represent the end of Jesus' life or the spiritual birth of your life? Is it a symbol of a useless death or the hope of a new beginning?

Your answer will determine whether Jesus' finished work of redemption on the cross has truly become a reality in your life. Right now, can He make the same declaration about your life as He did on the cross? *"IT...IS...FINISHED!"*

10

EXALTATION

"Wherefore God hath highly exalted him."
Philippians 2:9a

When you travel the route of Calvary with Jesus, you begin to realize how abased Jesus became. You get a small sense of the poverty He experienced for our benefit. For example, as God, He gave up the glories of heaven to become a bondservant. As a servant, He humbled Himself to become a baby. As Creator of all, He came by way of a humble handmaiden and a manger. As a baby, He was at the mercy of fallen humanity. As a boy ready to enter manhood, He was still subjected to His parents. On the day of His water baptism, He submitted Himself to John the Baptist. In the wilderness He came into obedience to the Word of God instead of His needs and rights.

His abasement continued as He walked a narrow path of self-denial during His ministry. As He told one enthusiastic, would-be follower, *"Foxes have holes, and birds of the air have nests; but the Son of man hath nowhere to lay his head" (Luke 9:58).*

Jesus continued this humble route up to the end of His life. He emptied Himself of the essence of His humanity in Gethsemane and gave up His life on the cross. He was placed in a tomb, while tasting the bitter cup of death, and walked in the midst of the bowels of the earth, preaching to the captives.[1]

Psalm 22:6 describes Jesus' abasement with this prophetic statement, *"I am a worm, and no man."* Jesus allowed Himself to become a worm in status. Unlike a snake, a worm must accept any abuse given to it because it has no power to fight back. If a snake senses danger, it rises up to protect its existence. This is what self-will does in man. Jesus actually gave up His right to fight back when He became subject to the will of the Father. Like the worm, He accepted the abuse of men that ended in His crucifixion.

Because Jesus allowed Himself to be brought to such depths of depravation, God highly exalted Him. This simply means that Jesus was exalted to the highest place. The Apostle Paul put Jesus' exaltation in this perspective in *Colossians 2:10, "And ye are complete in him, which is the head of all principality and power."*

It is incredible to think how far Jesus abased Himself, only to be exalted to the highest place. This is why the whole essence of Jesus' teaching is that of self-abasement. He is calling His followers to take on the status of a worm. However, before this task can be accomplished, they must humble themselves.

In order to humble ourselves, each of us must become harmless as a dove and innocent as a lamb in the midst of wolves.[2] We ultimately must reach great depths of depravation through self-denial and loss before we will truly realize the heights of God. Andrew Murray said it best, "Just as water ever seeks and fills the lowest place, so the moment God finds you abased and empty, His glory and power flow in."

We must follow the same path of judgments as Jesus did to realize the glory of God. In the Garden of Gethsemane, our

---

[1] Acts 2:27
[2] Matthew 10:16; Romans 8:36

humanity will only be poured out as we exchange our will for the will of God. At Gabbatha, our flesh must lose in order for God's perfect plan to have its way. At Golgotha, the total essence of our life (rights and identity) must be offered up in order to possess the life of Jesus.

In short, we must deny self and pick up our cross just as Jesus did. For Jesus, the cross represented death, but ultimately it lifted Him up for the whole world to consider in regards to the matter of one's eternal destination. The cross guaranteed death, but in the end there is resurrected life.

Watchman Nee made this statement about resurrection, "Hence a life which bears the marks of death and yet is alive is called resurrection."[3] Resurrection can only occur when a death has taken place. The purpose of death is to rid a person of the things associated with the first Adam. If there is no death of the old man, then there will be no resurrection of the new and everlasting life.[4]

The cross and resurrection walk hand in hand. It is in death that the cross is able to lift up the humble in power, exalt those who are abased to a place of glory, and bring resurrection power to the lost and hopeless.

The problem with some Christians is that they avoid the cross. They like the idea of it, but refuse to become identified with it. They appreciate the salvation it offers, but stop short of understanding it as a necessary aspect of our Christian life that each of us must personally embrace. They accept the brokenness it wrought in Jesus' body that produced healing, but shun the reality that they must be personally broken as well to experience spiritual wholeness of heart, mind, and soul. They readily embrace the fact that Jesus became a worm in status as He accepted man's blows, but refuse to take on a status of a "nobody" so Christ can become a "somebody" in their lives.

---

[3] Christ the Sum of All Spiritual Things, pg. 27
[4] Romans 6:3-10

The cross was designed to strike fatal blows to the essence of the old disposition of man. This is the only instrument that is able to humble each of us in order to bring us to a place of exaltation. On the cross the flesh dies, pride is silenced and dethroned, rights are crossed out, and earthly identity is lost. As a result, *I* no longer live, but Christ now lives in me.

As He lives in me, I am being exalted with Him into high places. In a sense, I have now become an empty shell that can only echo the awesomeness of Christ in His beauty. I am a worthless vessel that has been made valuable because the presence and fragrance of Christ fills my life. In the scheme of things, I have become a "nobody," but in the kingdom of God I am now an heir to a spiritual inheritance that is complete because Jesus is the sum of all spiritual things.[5]

To experience the resurrected life of Christ, I must first be broken. The cross causes brokenness, and each of us must be broken in order for God to put us back together for His use and glory. The cross consumes, and we must become lost in it so we can find our life and identity in Christ. The cross rids us of a past that can now be left buried, vanity that can be sealed up, and worldly pursuits that have lost their attraction in the grave. It is in such an environment that the very light of Jesus' resurrected life becomes a personal reality.

We know that the first four verses in *Philippians 2* describe how the attitude of Christ will express itself in our lives. *Philippians 2:6-8* describe how a humble, meek attitude expressed itself in Jesus' life. Let us consider the following table on the next page to show how the attitude of Christ manifested itself in His humanity and how it will make itself apparent in the lives of believers.

---

[5] Galatians 2:20; Ephesians 2:6; 2 Corinthians 2:15-16; 4:7; Ephesians 1:9-14

Jesus	Man
Deity: Adjusted His nature to take on a different disposition.	**Humility:** Neglect personal pride through self-denial.
Disposition: He became a servant. He became poor on our behalf.	**Submission:** Lining up to the ways of God to ensure righteousness.
Fashioned: Was shaped as man without sin, became God's sin offering for each of us.	**Death:** Death to self—personal plans, to be made into His righteousness.
Humanity: He became our example of the righteous man.	**Life:** Death allows the life of Jesus to be established in us.
Obedient: Out of obedience He became the sin offering.	**Servant:** It is at this point we will become a true servant of God.

In light of this, is it any wonder that God resists those who hold onto their pride?[6] The proud want the best for their lives but refuse to bend their necks to allow the yoke of the cross to break and discipline them.

The **conceited** want to know about the things of God, but will not allow their own knowledge to become dung in order to know the person of Jesus Christ. The **arrogant** want to be distinguished in some way by the cross, but will not submit to brokenness because they are unwilling to lose all control and say over their lives. The **self-centered** want the benefits of Christ, but will not give up their unyielding rights to know the real authority they can have in Him. The **self-serving** want to be associated with the cross, but do not want to be identified to the life of the cross, which is Christ living alongside, within, and

---

[6] James 4:6

through them. As a result, the proud will be brought down to spiritual ruin and destruction because they lack the resurrected power of Christ's life.

Do you have the mark of death on you? Have you avoided becoming identified with the cross? If you have, God will never be able to exalt you in the life He has prepared for you. As Jesus said in *Luke 18:14b, "for every one that exalteth himself shall be abased, and he that humbleth himself shall be exalted."*

11

OH, WHAT A NAME!

"...are given him a name which is above every name:
That at the name of Jesus every knee should bow..."
Philippians 2:9-10a

What can you say about the name of Jesus? How can you begin to grasp the meaning behind this glorious name? *Isaiah 9:6* gives us a special insight into Jesus' name. *"For unto us a child is born, unto us a son is given: and the government shall be upon his shoulder: and his **name** shall be called Wonderful, Counselor, the Mighty God, the everlasting Father, the Prince of Peace."* (Emphasis added.)

According to *Strong's Exhaustive Concordance,* the word "name" in both *Isaiah* and *Philippians* have the same meaning.[1] It indicates a distinct person, but it actually goes one step further to imply this person's mark, and also denotes their honor, authority, and character.

It's vital to realize it was the character of Jesus that determined His name, not the other way around. In other words, Jesus did not have to live up to His name like some of us do, but rather His name describes Him. Jesus came into this world with honor as the only begotten Son of God, with authority as the Son of Man, and displaying the character of the spiritual, heavenly

_____

[1] See #8034 and 3686

man as brought out in *1 Corinthians 15:45-50*. In fact, the names in Isaiah accredited to Jesus revealed to the world His identity long before He ever entered into it as a child in the manger. The names in Isaiah can be summarized into one glorious name: **JESUS.**

The first name given to Him is *Wonderful.* Wonderful describes someone who is not only wondrous in every way but is unexplainable. Let's ponder this reality for just a moment. Can any one word paint a picture of Jesus' majesty? Could all the words in the world begin to explain His glory? Of course not! The Apostle Paul called Jesus, God's unspeakable gift.[2] In *Revelation 1*, we see that John's encounter with Jesus not only overwhelmed him, but he was also overcome by the reality of His Lord.

Jesus' name should bring such awe to us as we realize that He cannot be explained, comprehended, or worshipped in the manner to which He is worthy. We should always be ready to bow our necks in humility, our knees in submission, and our hearts in adoration to the One who is beyond description.

Obviously, in His wonder, Jesus is beautiful! His beauty is proclaimed by creation, outshines the streets of gold in heaven, and is as immeasurable as the heavens above. How we need to worship Him in spirit and truth![3] *Psalm 8:1* and *29:2* say it best, *"O LORD our Lord, how excellent is thy name in all the earth! Who hast set thy glory above the heavens?.... Give unto the LORD the glory due unto his name; worship the LORD in the beauty of holiness."*

The next name in Isaiah's lineup is *Counselor.* As our Counselor, Jesus serves as our *wisdom. James 3:17* describes Jesus' attributes as our wisdom. He is first of all pure. In other words, there is no uncleanness in Him. His heart is perfect towards us. His intentions concerning our best are honorable,

---

[2] 2 Corinthians 9:15
[3] John 4:24

and are freely given to those who believe, love, and obey Him. His commitment towards our spiritual welfare is of the highest quality. He proved all this when He went to the cross as our substitute.

Since Jesus is pure towards us in every way, we can trust His intervention and counsel in our lives. The problem is that very few trust and regard His counsel; therefore, they never benefit from Him as their Counselor.

The second virtue of His wisdom is that it is peaceable. In other words, He is not aggressive or demanding. As our Counselor, He is meek and humble. His desire is simple; He wants to take the unbearable yokes off our necks and put them on Himself, making our load light. He wants to take our overwhelming burdens and replace them with the light burden of simply trusting and loving Him.

Next, His wisdom is gentle. He is mild in His approach to those who are wounded because He is the great Physician who heals the broken lives and hearts of people. His goal is to bring a sweet fragrance to each of our lives, a healing balm to our souls, and an anointing to our spirits. *Song of Solomon 1:3* gives us this special insight, *"Because of the savour of thy good ointments thy name is as ointment poured forth, therefore do the virgins love thee."*

Jesus is gentle—patient with us in our frailties and longsuffering in our rebellion. After all, He is not willing that any perish but that all come to repentance.[4]

In His infinite wisdom, Jesus can be entreated. He can actually be persuaded because of His love to listen to our greatest concerns. He is attentive in hearing the silent cries of our heart, and will move heaven and earth to answer our deepest desires.

---

[4] 2 Peter 3:9

The persuasion that can entreat Jesus can only occur within two distinct boundaries. First, we must pray in His name. It is important to point out there is no power in the *name* of Jesus, but in the *Person* of Jesus. When we pray in His name, we are praying according to His Person or character.

The Word describes Jesus' body as a veil that was torn. This is symbolic of our right to boldly enter into the Most Holy Place. The Most Holy Place points to intimate communion with God, while the concept of a torn veil reminds us that such communion can only take place through Jesus because of what He accomplished on the cross. We are told in *Hebrews 4:16, "Let us therefore come boldly unto the throne of grace that we may obtain mercy, and find grace to help in time of need."*

Jesus is the door we must enter into through prayer. To exercise our right we must knock on the door to gain entrance. For example, when I invite someone to my home and they stand outside my door knocking to receive entrance, I know that they are responding to my invitation.

Jesus has sent many invitations forth to those who are His. His servants are the ones who bring the invitations. However, each of us must respond and come and knock on the door He has provided for us to benefit from the life He offers. As the Spirit cries out on His behalf, *"Come. And let him that heareth say, Come. And let him that is athirst come. And whosoever will, let him take the water freely" (Revelation 22:17).*

Our Lord is also the gate. We must enter through this gate of prayer to embrace a new and rich life. We each must understand that these three entrances represent the facets of Jesus' character. As the veil, He allows us entrance because His blood has bought us; therefore, we have the right to become children of God.

As our door, He gives entrance by way of who He is and must be to us personally. To enter by way of the door shows we are in agreement with Him as our only way, truth, and life. Keep in mind there is only one door, and its entrance is narrow.

The gate means that since we have entered by way of who He is, now we can walk according to His mind, heart, and will for our lives. This is the second qualification to ensure answered prayers: God can only answer prayers according to His will. We cannot understand His will unless we enter by way of the door and pass through the veil.

Many prayers go amiss because they are not done in Jesus, according to His character, and in line with His perfect will. As a result, we miss much godly insight. Keep in mind that it is in our prayer life that the greatest counseling can actually take place.

Jesus' wisdom is full of mercy and good fruits. Let me ask you, have you ever been around an unfeeling counselor? Such a counselor has no patience with your struggles, compassion for your wounds, and no love to cover your faults. These counselors make you feel like a failure before any healing can take place. And, what are the fruits of such meetings? They produce a fleshly response of condemnation and hopelessness.

Jesus knows everything about us. There is not one wound hidden from His sight. He knows every struggle and every failure. Regardless of the challenge, His invitation is the same, *"Come to Me just the way you are."*

As our counselor, Jesus is not partial. We often fail to recognize this wonderful quality about our committed Counselor. He considers each case individually. He holds up no rulers by which to measure us. He has no favorites that will put us in competition with others. He considers us without conditions or expectations. He sees our potential, desires to work with our failures, heal our wounds, and bring hope to our hearts.

Finally, as our wisdom, He does not possess any hypocrisy. He has no mixture in His commitment, love, and intention for us. He is the same today as He was yesterday and will be tomorrow.[5] He does not say one thing and turn around and do something totally opposite. He does not toy with emotions or flatter anyone with useless words. He is true in every way to what He says, knows, and does.

Next, Isaiah tells us Jesus is to be known as *"The Mighty God."* This tells us that Jesus is God and in His deity He is mighty and strong. "Mighty" implies that He is a Champion of champions.[6] Jesus, as Man, ran the longest race, hit every mark, tackled the greatest enemies, wrestled the most powerful foe, carried the heaviest weight on His shoulders, and jumped the widest gulf in the spiritual realm (the one that existed between life and death).

As mighty, He proved to be the greatest warrior. In fact, the great warrior Joshua took his shoes off in the presence of Jesus. This showed that Joshua recognized the presence of someone who was worthy of all adoration and recognition.[7]

Jesus ultimately proved to be a mighty warrior when He won the war for the souls of man on the cross and in the grave. He subdued the enemy of death and took the power out of sin.[8]

Jesus is also mighty because He is an overcomer. In *John 16:33,* Jesus declared that He had overcome the world. The world is made up of the lust of the flesh, pride of life, and the lust of the eyes.[9] Jesus overcame the world by subduing His flesh, putting all pride under His feet, and looking upward to keep His focus in the right place instead of around or downward.

If Jesus overcame all of our enemies in the flesh, won all the battles that raged over our souls on the cross, and endured all the obstacle courses in His humanity in order to win the prize of eternity for you and me, can we do any less? The Apostle John

---

[5] Hebrews 13:8
[6] Strong's Exhaustive Concordance of the Bible, #1368
[7] Joshua 5:13-15
[8] 1 Corinthians 15:54-57
[9] 1 John 2:15-17

answers that question in *1 John 5:3* and *4. "For whatsoever is born of God overcometh the world: and this is the victory that overcometh the world, even our faith."*

It will indeed be glorious when Jesus appears in the eastern skies as the KING OF KINGS, LORD OF LORDS![10] There will be no doubt when He makes this appearance that He is indeed *The Mighty God!*

Isaiah tells us the next name of Jesus is *The Everlasting Father.* Everlasting means "perpetual, ongoing, and eternal". We know that Jesus is eternal because of His deity. In *Revelation 1,* Jesus stated, *"I am Alpha and Omega, the first and the last."*

In His confrontation with the Jews, Jesus made this statement in *John 8:58, "Verily, verily, I say unto you, before Abraham was, I am."* The prophet *Daniel* called Jesus, "the Ancient of days." Everything about Jesus is eternal. His life in us is ongoing. His ministry on our behalf is perpetual, and His love unending. There are no limits to His mercies for they are new every day, and no boundaries to His grace where sin has once reigned and now has been destroyed by His great work on the cross. He, in fact, is the sum of all spiritual things, and without Him there is nothing that is of eternal value, significant in meaning, substantial in purpose, or important to our spiritual welfare. He is all in all![11]

Jesus is our Father in a wondrous way. It is in the heart of the Godhead to be our Father. A devoted father takes responsibility for the welfare of his children. He protects them like a hen does her chicks, and watches over them as an eagle from a place of authority. His ears are open to their every cry, his heart to their every need, and his arms ready to enfold them in the times of fear and hurt.

It is the heart of God to have this type of relationship with you and me. Each person of the Godhead is committed to ensure this

---

[10] Matthew 24:27; Revelation 19:11-16
[11] Lamentations 3:22-23; Daniel 7:9; Romans 5:20; Colossians 3:11

relationship, which has been made available for everyone. Jesus went to the cross to secure our rights as children. The Holy Spirit through conviction and His indwelling presence signifies our adoption. The adoption allows us to know our rights as children of God and to realize the intimacy made available with the Father through Jesus Christ.[12]

Each person of the Godhead also ensures this intimate relationship is maintained. Jesus intercedes for us as the High Priest; the Holy Spirit guides us into all truth and a life that is beyond reproach. The Father keeps His heart open to embrace us with His presence in the Most Holy place of communion at all times.[13]

As children of God, we each now have the right to commune with Him. After communion with God, we will come out knowing that God is beyond words. We will become overwhelmed that His face, as reflected in Jesus Christ, is beautiful and beyond description.

The final title in Isaiah is *the Prince of Peace.* Jesus is the sole source of our peace. He gained this title because only by His shed blood on the cross can we now have peace with our Creator.[14]

Sin has made mankind an enemy of God, and rebellion has caused lost humanity to reject God's authority in their lives. This conflict has robbed people of peace of mind and causes great turmoil and restlessness in their wandering souls. It literally destroys their spirits, and makes them part of the walking dead who aimlessly travel through this world as vagabonds or fugitives.

As Jesus stated, He came to give peace, not as the world gives, but a peace that is lasting even in the midst of great

---

[12] Romans 8:14-17
[13] John 14:6, 26; Hebrews 7:24-26
[14] John 14:27; Colossians 1:20

trials.[15] This peace finds it source in a relationship with God through the second Person of the Godhead.

Jesus is not only the ruler of peace, but He is also the essence of peace. His meekness overcomes aggression, His lowliness silences competition, His humility ends conflicts, and His submission stops adversaries in their tracks. He can bring peace to a weary mind, troubled heart, and hopeless soul. He can still the storms raging in our lives, calm the swells ready to shipwreck us, and halt and defeat any advancement from our enemies.

In logical order, each of Jesus' names in Isaiah leads to the following name and upholds its meaning. For example, Jesus Christ can only be *the Prince of Peace* in our lives when we have been established in that intimate *Father-child* relationship with God.[16]

As Jesus becomes more real to us in this intimate relationship, we will begin to know Him as *The Mighty God* who is our Champion, Warrior, and Overcomer in every area of our life. As His eternal, all-powerful character comes out in victory as God, we will be able to recognize and trust Him as our *Counselor* who actually gave up heaven so He could become identified with us in every way. As His commitment, love, wisdom, and insight penetrate every area of our lives, we will begin to see how *Wonderful* He is, ultimately causing Him to become a priceless gem that we will sacrifice all to possess.

To me it is humbling that Isaiah describes Jesus with five terms. Is it any wonder that the name of *"Jesus"* has only five letters in it? Is this similarity only coincidental? Hardly! The number "five" denotes God's grace.

The work of redemption on our behalf and in our lives has been completely wrought by God. This work is motivated by His love, and is an act of total grace on His part. Therefore, we

---

[15] John 14:27
[16] Matthew 5:9

cannot take credit for our salvation, for it is a free gift of God. We cannot take glory for any godliness in our lives because it belongs to God who freely gives it as we humble ourselves and submit to His work. We cannot receive any applause for sanctification in our lives, for only the Spirit can sanctify.[17] The eternal work in us is of God, and the abounding love, which compels us, belongs to Him. Obviously, we are nothing outside of Jesus Christ. His life should be consuming us in such a way that He alone will be left standing.

Has Jesus become *Wonderful, Counselor, The Mighty God, The Everlasting Father, and the Prince of Peace* in your life? Has He become so indescribable to you that the whisper of His very name ends in worship or adoration? Has He become so precious to you that His very name causes your heart to leap with joy, your neck to bend in humility, your knees to fall to the ground, and your arms to reach up not only to touch the hem of His garment, but to be touched by the reality of His majesty or glory?

Is the name *"Jesus"* a magic word to you that you repeat as if a mantra to invoke some response from an unseen force or behind the name is there a real person whom you actually love with all your heart, soul, mind, and might? Do you use the name of *"Jesus"* to display some kind of power play over the demonic world, or does the demonic world shake because you know Him? Is the name of *"Jesus"* a byword you use to appear religious, or the name of the One who is your Lord, Savior, and Redeemer of your soul?

Jesus' name has meaning because of who He is. As already stated, the name *"Jesus"* in and by itself means nothing. It is the Person of Jesus Christ who brings His name meaning. Let us not worship a name, idea, or concept, but rather let us worship Him, the Person, in His unending majesty.

---

[17] Romans 15:16

Know this: It is only after we worship our Lord in spirit and truth that we will begin to understand the beauty of His name. As His beauty unfolds before our very eyes, we will then be able to declare, *"Jesus, o-o-o-oh what a name!"* Let's praise His holy name!

12

HE IS LORD!

*"And that every tongue should confess
that Jesus Christ is Lord,
to the glory of God the Father."*
Philippians 2:11

I have often been overwhelmed and humbled to think that one day every knee shall bow before Jesus. Think about it for a second. Every person who has ever mocked and defied God, every cult leader and each of their members, every atheist and all those who have worshipped Satan, along with Satan and his cohorts, will be brought before the Son of God.

It is possible that we as believers will witness an event that should have taken place on earth in the life of every person. Every stiff neck will bow, every son of Belial will fall to the ground, every wicked leader will be brought low, and every hater of God will be brought humbled before Jesus Christ. It will be at this time we will watch them bow in homage before the King of kings and Lord of lords.

Not only will they bow, but they will also open their mouths. These various mouths which have spoken blasphemies, mocked the things of God, falsely accused His saints as well as cursed His holy character, and used His name in vain will find themselves confessing a truth they had rejected in their hearts and denounced in their natural lives. They will confess that Jesus Christ is **LORD**!

During this time justice will be realized; every persecuted, mocked saint vindicated; and Jesus Christ officially exalted over those who had refused to receive Him into their lives on the basis of who He is. What a glorious time that will be! However, it will also be a sorrowful time as these lost souls begin to realize they really missed it, and are about to reap His wrath.

Matthew 7:21-23 talks about people who will argue with Jesus' rejection of them because they did deeds in His name. However, such deeds that were performed for the doers' own personal vainglory, will not be considered acceptable to God; rather they will be considered a source of iniquity before Him.

Over the years I have met many people who insisted on erroneous beliefs. In one case, a woman became very angry with me when I stepped on her religious idols. I remember thinking that on judgment day she will be repentant and feeling sorry that she chose to disbelieve the evidence and warnings about her idolatrous beliefs. As I was pondering this thought, the Lord revealed to me that this lady will not be repentant on judgment day, but angry that I was right and she was wrong.

It dawned on me that on judgment day there will be no place for repentance—just tears of self-pity, anger that will be stirred up by the fires of hell, and fear of judgment, but not of God.

I have tried to imagine what it will be like for those who oppose God to find themselves at this place. I am not saying my conclusions are right, but the scenario has posed a thought-provoking picture for me. For example, some of these people actually believed that heaven was a sure thing because they have been decent people. They did not murder or rob. They didn't curse or commit adultery, but they also have never recognized their need for Jesus either.

As these individuals begin to see Jesus' nail-pierced hands, they will find their miserable fig leaves of self-righteousness falling away, revealing spiritual nakedness and shame. They neglected God's salvation, and now are coming face-to-face with the One who held an insignificant place in their lives. They will probably be surprised that Jesus is unable to declare their names before the Father.[1]

Others will be surprised because they really believed Jesus did not exist. He was an imaginary crutch for the weak and a figment of the imagination to those who clung to Him. The biblical account of Him, in their opinion, was nothing more than a nice fable. Therefore, all that such intellectual individuals were capable of doing was to compare this apparent "myth" to another Santa Claus, tooth fairy, or Easter bunny and nothing more, right? Wrong! Now His very presence will mock and call them fools.[2]

You will see the sons of Belial as well. They worshipped the world, laughed at decency, and clung to pleasure. They refused to give up their immoral lifestyles, drugs. and ungodly pursuits. They hated with a vengeance and took pride in their works of darkness. They were predators within a vulnerable, helpless society. They loved highs, loathed honesty, and hated God.

Now they find themselves standing in front of the One they hated. This time they stand in silence, for they have no power to do anything else. In their hearts they still mock Him, and in their minds they are still shaking their fists at Him, but they are about to do something so contrary to their previous lives: They are about to bow before Him.

I must also consider those who became predators among Jesus' flock. They masked their self-serving agendas behind His name. They had been part of the miracles and movements that had actually allowed them to become a replacement for Jesus in many people's lives. However, in their deluded minds that small fact could not be held against them. They were simply opportunists that gave God's people what they wanted: a

---

[1] Hebrew 2:3; Matthew 10:32
[2] Psalm 14:1; Matthew 10:33

magnificent show. They had learned to become professional orators in the midst of these religious people who wanted to have their ears tickled and their flesh fed. Surely, Jesus can't blame them for making a living, even if it was at the expense of His flock, right?[3]

Wrong! These people used God to merchandise the souls of men for their own perverted, self-serving means. They are going to be held accountable to an even higher degree, and something in the air will cause them to tremble in fear. They used Jesus' name like a magic wand, but now they will be face-to-face with Him. The mask they had cleverly hidden behind will now take the shape of a Person who will look into their very souls. Everything will be stripped away from them.

Their self-importance will begin to crumble, and their religious works will start to mock them as reality dawns upon them. For years they had seduced people to worship and adore them while they cleverly hid behind Jesus' name and reputation for their own gain. But now they begin to realize the name of Jesus belonged to a real Person. It was this Person who alone was worthy of all worship, and they are about to fall down before Him to take their rightful place—at His feet, while their own devoted followers look on, stunned, fearful, and accusing.[4]

There will also be the evil leaders who supported Satan. They advocated abortions, alternative lifestyles, tyrannical laws, and godless philosophies that would undermine the moral laws of God. They put heavy burdens on His people in the name of tolerance and democracy. In fact, they did everything to destroy the moral fabric of the nations, countries, kingdoms, and families.

They had made plans to bring in the one-world government. They had come so far only to be stopped on some battlefield or in some political arena by an unseen hand. They had gloried in

---

[3] 2 Timothy 4:3; Jeremiah 23:23-40; Ezekiel 34:2-7; Matthew 23:12-36
[4] John 2:14-16; 2 Peter 2:3

their power, abused their authority, and toyed with lives as if people were nothing more than a cheap commodity.

Now they stand in the presence of One who holds all power and authority. They thought they were the ones in control, but now they begin to realize that they had been nothing more than pawns in the hands of Satan, used to ultimately fulfill the plans of God. He was the One who had the unseen hand that determined their limitations and destruction. He had been in control all along and had actually laughed at their foolish plans.[5]

Jesus Christ is real, and everyone who denied His existence with their mouth, lifestyles, or pursuits will face Him in the end. These people will bow and declare that it is Jesus Christ who is Lord. As the Apostle Paul declared *in 1 Corinthians 8:6*, He alone holds this title or position.

Most likely when these disloyal subjects declare that Jesus is Lord, they will seal their own fate. It is a known fact that subjects who do not recognize the authority of their King and Lord are traitors. This is an act of high treason that demands death. It is important to realize that when these people proclaim Jesus as Lord, they are also recognizing who He is, and what part He should have played in their lives.

Since Jesus is our Lord, we need to become His bondservants. A bondservant is a servant who serves out of love. In fact, a bondservant will abandon a normal life to become a devoted servant to the master.

As Lord, Jesus' deity is once again confirmed. *Isaiah 45:21c* makes this statement, *"Am not I the LORD? And there is no God else beside me; a just God and a Saviour; there is none beside me."* Since Jesus is God, He does deserve our worship and adoration. There should not be any divided loyalties in our lives because there is only one true God.

---

[5] Psalm 2:1-4

This Scripture also shows us that as our Lord, He is our Savior. He is the only One who can save us. The problem with many Christians is that we see Jesus as our Savior, but not as our Lord. He comes in one package, and we must accept every facet of His character to experience the fullness of His salvation. Keep in mind that it is because Jesus is God that He is able to save us. But, in order for us to possess His life, He must become the Lord of our lives.

As Lord, Jesus is also our Shepherd who has purchased us with His blood; therefore, He owns us. Since we belong to Him, we have no personal rights. Because we are His sheep, He is responsible for our welfare. However, to experience this type of leadership we must follow Him in obedience.

To follow Jesus means we will begin to know Him in an intimate way. As we get to know Him, we will be able to recognize His voice, even among voices of those who are not our real shepherd.

As Lord, Jesus is also our strength and song according to *Deuteronomy 15:2.* Obviously, Jesus is an abiding place we can run into to find everything we have need of to live a godly life. In fact, Jesus is all in all. He is the sum of all spiritual things.

I was reminded not too long ago that Christians make a mistake in separating God from His abilities and promises. For example, we claim one of God's promises, and then we expect Him to meet us at our need or request. The truth is, Jesus is the essence of the promise we are claiming, and we need to come to Him to realize it.

If we are hungry, He is the bread of Life. If we are thirsty, He is the Giver of Living Water. All we need to do is come, abide in Him, and fellowship with Him to begin to partake of the abundance of His life.[6]

---

[6] John 6:35; 7:37-39; 10:10; 14:13-14; 15:1-8; Hebrews 7:24-26

He is our hope; therefore, if we need hope, all we need to do is simply come to Him. Maybe we need healing; He is the One who heals us, but we first must come to Him. If we need rest, He is our rest. If we need life, He is life. Everything we need to establish our spiritual lives can be found in a relationship with Jesus. Every promise can be realized when we come to Jesus in faith seeking Him. Every prayer can be answered when we come to Jesus, who serves as our door of intercession.[7]

In order to realize all that Jesus has for us, we must come to Him as bondservants. We must make Him our Lord and learn to follow Him into the life He has for us. As a servant, we need not only to serve Him, but also to abide with Him. As Ruth with Boaz, we need to lie at His feet, putting ourselves in His care. We need to get up clinging to Him in expectancy of experiencing every day with the One we love.

It is in this type of setting that a servant begins to learn the heart of their master. In this type of arena, a servant will become sensitive to the desires of the master. In this type of situation, the relationship can grow into a powerful friendship. [8]

The truth is that Jesus wants us to become His close friends. We can only experience this intimate friendship with Him when we become a recipient of His salvation and a humble servant in His kingdom.

Let me ask you, have you made Jesus your Lord and King, or is He simply just your Savior? Has Jesus become all in all to you, or is He just a name you use for fire insurance? Who is Jesus to you? These are the most important questions you must ask yourself.

Jesus must become everything to you that has been clearly established in the Word. Do not fail this test because your eternal destination will be determined along this line.

---

[7] Luke 4:18; John 14:6; Colossians 1:27
[8] Ruth 3:1-12; John 15:15

253

My prayer for all of you is that you have already bowed your neck in recognition that you are a sinner in need of a Savior. After you have bowed your neck, I hope you bend your knees before Jesus who is not only your Savior, but who is also God Incarnate, the One who deserves your worship and adoration. After you have bowed your knees in worship, I pray that you have opened your mouth and confessed before the kingdom of darkness and the kingdom of Light that Jesus Christ is **your Lord.** This gives notice to the kingdom of darkness that you are going to serve Jesus, for you now belong to Him. Such a confession will bring praises forth from the kingdom of light as all those around His throne bow before Him in agreement with you.

If you have not done this, you need to before it is too late. It is better to confess Jesus as Lord now, rather than later. Now ensures eternal life, while later could end up mocking you for your foolishness, and branding you as the worst kind of traitor to the King of kings and the Lord of lords.

In Conclusion

This ends the incredible journey we have been taking in this small book. We started out with Jesus Christ giving up His glory to take on the form of a servant and to be fashioned as a man, but who ended being exalted as Lord over all. We followed Jesus from eternity into a manger and up a road to Calvary. We caught glimpses of Him in glory, heard His cries in a garden, and watched Him give up His spirit on a cross. We followed Him through the midst of man's depravity right into the grave, only to discover the ultimate hope of man, Christ Jesus in us, the hope of glory.

We also stood at Bethlehem to rejoice with the angels at His birth, only to wait for Him to emerge after years of obscurity and preparation. We followed Him with expectancy as He walked among humanity and touched the people with power. We marveled at His teachings, cheered over His confrontation with the religious leaders, wept at the cross, and rejoiced at the empty tomb, only to worship at His feet as our risen Lord and Savior.

My, what a journey it has been! I have taken this journey every time I read through one of the Gospels. However, *Philippians* continues to remind me of something I sometimes miss while reading the account in the Gospels. The Gospels show me how He suffered and died, but Jesus' glorious resurrection always overshadows the tremendous price He paid to obtain our salvation. *Philippians* reminds me of that price, but it goes one step further.

This epistle actually shows me the great price He paid in light of His attitude. Even though the price was great and entailed more than we could ever comprehend in our lifetime, His attitude about it all says the most about His commitment to each of us. *He actually thought it not robbery* to go from glory to depravity, from worship to mockery, from praise to a cross, from miracles to a grave, from the depths of hell to resurrection power, and from servitude to Lordship. To me this attitude not only tells me of His humility, submission, and obedience, but also of His love, mercy, and grace.

Won't you agree with me now? Oh, what a Lord we have! Let us praise and worship Him in His majesty, beauty, and glory! Let us thank Him for all He accomplished for us yesterday on the cross as Savior, today as our Lord and High Priest, and tomorrow as our Hope of glory! Let us lift Him up in our praises, worship, commitment, love, and life for the whole world to see just <u>how wonderful He is</u>!

Bibliography

Strong's Exhaustive Concordance of the Bible; James Strong; World Bible Publishers

Webster's New Collegiate Dictionary; © 1976 by G. & C. Merriam Co.

Evidence That Demands A Verdict; by Josh McDowell ©1972, 1979 by Campus Crusade for Christ

Jewish Faith and the New Covenant; by Ruth Specter Lascelle; © 1980

Daily Thoughts for Disciples; Oswald Chambers, © 1990 by Oswald Chambers Publishing Association.

Vine's Expository Dictionary of Biblical Words, ©1985 by Thomas Nelson, Inc., Publishers

Smith's Bible Dictionary; William Smith, L.L.D.; Thomas Nelson Publishers

A Glimpse At Early Christian Church Life; Tertullian, ©1991 by David W. Bercot

The Pilgrim Church; E. H. Broadbent, © 1999; Gospel Folio Press

Christ, the Sum of All Spiritual Things, Watchman Nee, © 1973 by Christian Fellowship Publishers, Inc.

Great People of the Bible and How They Lived, © 1974 The Reader's Digest Association, Inc.

In the Footsteps of Jesus, © 1997 by Bruce Marchiano

Bringing Sons Into Glory & Making All Things New, © 1990 by Oswald Chambers Publications Association

Bible in the News, February 1999 Issue

God's Will: Our Dwelling Place, Andrew Murray

Lectures on the Book of Acts, by H. A. Ironside, 18th printing 1982

Other books by Rayola Kelley:

Volume Six: Developing Our Christian Life
The Many Faces of Christianity
*Possessing Our Souls
Experiencing the Christian Life
The Power of Our Testimonies
*The Victorious Journey

Devotions
Devotions of the Heart: Books One and Two
Daily Food for the Soul: Books One and Two

Gentle Shepherd Ministries Devotion Series:
Being a Child of God
Disciplining the Strength of our Youth
Coming to Full Age

Nugget Books:
Nuggets From Heaven
More Nuggets From Heaven
Heavenly Gems
More Heavenly Gems
Heavenly Treasures
More Heavenly Treasures

Gentle Shepherd Ministries Series:

The Christian Life Series
What Matter Is This?
The Challenge of It
The Reality of It

The Leadership Series
Overcoming
A Matter of Authority and Power
The Dynamics of True Leadership

Books By:
Jeannette Haley
Books co-authored with Rayola Kelley:
Hidden Manna (original)
The Many Faces of Christianity (Volume 6)
Post to Post 3: Meditations Along the Way
Post to Post 4: Inspirations Along the Way
Post to Post 5: Collecting Gems Along the Way

Other Books:
Rose of Light, Thorn of Darkness
Interview In Hell}
Interview On Earth}
(Both Interview Books are now in one book
Angelus Assignments)
The Pig and I
Reflections of Wonder (Devotional)

Children's Books:
Little Stories for Little People
Traveler's Tales
The Adventures of Zack and Mira
The Adventures of Paul and Dana
(A House on the Beach)
The Monster of Mystery Valley

*Books that have been separated from the volumes and are now available under their own titles.

www.ingramcontent.com/pod-product-compliance
Lightning Source LLC
Chambersburg PA
CBHW060013100426
42740CB00010B/1480